Lighthou
Engla

The North West
and Isle of Man

Tony Denton and Nicholas Leach

▲ The lighthouse at New Brighton guarding the entrance to the river Mersey.

◀ (Frontispiece) The lighthouse at the southern end of Walney Island, near Barrow in Furness.

Published by
Foxglove Media
Foxglove House
Shute Hill
Lichfield
Staffordshire WS13 8DB
England

Telephone 01543 673594
foxglove.media@btinternet.com

British Library Cataloguing in Publication Data. A catalogue record for this book is available from the British Library.

ISBN 978 0 95645 601 4

Layout and design by
Nicholas Leach

Printed by Cromwell Press Group, Trowbridge

Contents

Lighthouse History

This book provides a comprehensive guide to the lighthouses and harbour lights around the coast of north-west England, from south to north starting with the lights on the Wirral and going to Cumbria, and on the Isle of Man, starting with Point of Ayre. This includes some notable architectural towers of historical significance, and the lighthouses are operated and maintained by a number of different organisations.

The Corporation of Trinity House is responsible for many of the lights on the English coast, including all the major ones, while the Northern Lighthouse Board operates many of the aids to navigation on the Isle of Man. The many significant small harbour lights, are operated by a variety of organisations, including local harbour boards. This introduction provides an overview of the development of lighthouse building and organisation in England and Scotland, examining the need for lights to mark the coasts around the Irish Sea, and looking at how aids to navigation have been provided in a historical context.

The first lights

Trading by sea has been a principal activity of all civilisations, yet moving goods and cargoes by water involves facing difficulties and dangers such as storms and bad weather, avoiding reefs, headlands, sandbanks and cliffs, and making safe passage into ports and harbours. The need for aids to navigation is therefore as old as trading by sea itself, and today modern lighthouses operated by nationally-managed bodies are supplemented by a plethora of small, locally-operated lights of varying sizes and range, around ports, harbours and estuaries.

The earliest aids to navigation were beacons or daymarks, sited near harbours or ports rather than on headlands or reefs, to help ships reach their destination safely. The earliest lighthouses were in the Mediterranean and the oldest such structure of which written records survive was that on the island of Pharos, off Alexandra on the northern coast of Egypt. The Pharos lighthouse, which stands 466ft tall, was built between 283BC and 247BC and stood until 1326.

The first navigational lights to be shown on England's north-west coast were in Cumbria at the port of Whitehaven and on St Bees headland. On the Isle of Man the first major lighthouses were at Point of Ayre and the Calf of Man, although a wooden light was attached to Derbyhaven Fort in 1650, the earliest example of a light being exhibited from a coastal lookout tower in Britain.

The development of lighthouses around the coasts of the British Isles mirrored the development of trade routes. Therefore vessels using the Irish Sea had to be warned of the dangers of the Isle of Man. However, as the major shipping channels did not pass either the Lancashire or Cumbrian coasts the need for major aids

to navigation in these areas was less critical than elsewhere.

Therefore the earliest British lights were on the south and south-east coast of England, built in the fifteenth and sixteenth centuries. By the seventeenth century lights were being erected along the east coast, to help guide colliers carrying coal from the north-east to London.

Colonial trade involving west coast ports, which expanded during the eighteenth and nineteenth centuries, came to be dominated by Liverpool. That port's expansion, which created a need for lighthouses, was considerable: for example, between 1772 and 1805 inward shipping, largely from America and the West Indies and including cargoes such as tobacco and sugar, increased from 77,000 tons to 331,000 tons, while the ignominious slave trade also played a significant role in aiding the port's expansion.

The dominance of the Liverpool trade is illustrated by the evidence of the lighthouse dues collected from ships passing the Smalls lighthouse in Pembrokeshire in 1831-32. From ships docking in Liverpool, £11,206 was collected, while trade to Swansea, Neath, Bristol and Beaumaris was only worth about £1,000 in dues to the Smalls from each port.

The Liverpool Town Council was the original port authority and managed the expansion of the port during the early nineteenth century. Both the

▲ Point of Ayre lighthouse on the northern tip of the Isle of Man was one of the first lighthouses built by the Northern Lighthouse Board.

▼ The old lighthouse at Leasowe is one of a number built in the eighteenth century to guide ships into the Mersey.

Lighthouse History

▶ The Tommy Legs light at Silloth, just off the town's west beach, pictured when in use as an operational light.

Council and its successor, the Mersey Docks and Harbour Board (created in 1858), established a significant number of lights on the approaches to the Mersey. The importance of Liverpool as a centre of shipping was demonstrated by the number of aids to navigation built along the channels into the river, with lights at one time shown from Formby, Bootle, New Brighton, Bidston Hill, Leasowe and Hoylake.

Trinity House

While organisations such as the Mersey Docks and Harbour Board operated lights at a local level, the building and maintenance of the major aids to navigation nationally was the responsibility of the Corporation of Trinity House. The exact origins of Trinity House are obscure, but probably date back to the early thirteenth century when groups of tradesmen, such as seamen, masters of merchant vessels and pilots, formed guilds to protect their interests.

One of the earliest such organisations was the Deptford Trinity House, which was granted a royal charter after its members petitioned Henry VIII to prohibit unqualified pilots on the Thames in 1513. Deptford was the main point of entry for the capital's trade, so pilotage duties were lucrative and Trinity House members wanted to retain their monopoly. A similar organisation was the Trinity House at Newcastle-upon-Tyne, which was

▼ The Low Light at Hoylake, which stood next to the lifeboat house, was used until 1908 and has since been demolished. It was one of a number built to mark the channels into the river Mersey.

responsible for aids to navigation on the Tyne from 1536, although no equivalent organisation existed on the north-west coast.

However, despite erecting some towers in East Anglia, during the seventeenth and eighteenth centuries Trinity House was generally reluctant to build lighthouses. Instead it encouraged entrepreneurs to consider building them as profit-making undertakings. As a result, private lighthouse ownership became relatively widespread during the seventeenth century as many towers were erected as private undertaking. Choosing the best position for a light, with sufficiently busy ports nearby

from where dues could be collected, was crucial for the light to yield a good return.

The lighthouse on the cliffs at St Bees Head was one for which Trinity House obtained a patent and which in turn was leased to a private individual, Thomas Lutwige. The headland was a danger to the many coastal vessels using the small harbours of Maryport, Whitehaven and Workington to the north, with dues levied at the rate of three-half pence a ton on cargo carried by vessels using these ports. The tower at St Bees carried a large metal grate into which he keepers tipped coal. When the tower was destroyed by fire in

▲ Rock lighthouse at New Brighton guards the entrance to the river Mersey, and is one of the river's best known landmarks.

◄ The small lighthouse at Hodbarrow Point dates from 1905 and was built by the local mining company to assist ships approaching the jetties to load iron ore.

Lighthouse History

This lighthouse at Whitehaven dates from 1841 and is one of four lights which had been built to mark this historic harbour.

for greed and lights were built around the coast on a somewhat haphazard basis. As a result, large areas of the coastline remained unlit, and by the nineteenth century, with the level of trade increasing as Britain's industry expanded, the situation had become unacceptable. Trinity House were given the responsibility for improving matters, and as the leases expired on privately-owned lighthouses the Corporation took over. In 1807 Trinity House assumed responsibility for the Eddystone lighthouse off Plymouth, and the next three decades saw great changes to lighthouse organisation in England and Wales.

These changes were formalised in 1836 with an Act of Parliament which gave Trinity House complete authority over lighthouses and made it the body to which others, including regional Trinity House organisations, had to apply for sanction of the position and character of lights. Although by this time the majority of

1822, it was the last coal light to be displayed in Britain.

Although a proliferation of unnecessary lights was prevented as a result of the involvement of private operation, private light owners gained a reputation

The high light at Fleetwood was one of two lights built in the nineteenth century to guide vessels into the port.

THE LIGHTHOUSE, ST. BEES HEAD, CUMBERLAND.

English lights were already controlled by Trinity House, the 1836 Act formally centralised lighthouse management.

Once all the private lighthouses had been taken over, Trinity House gradually assumed control of lighthouse maintenance and oversaw the construction of many significant towers in the nineteenth century. During the great period of lighthouse construction between 1870 and 1900, Victorian engineers and designers constructed and modernised at least fifty stations and built new rock towers. Lighthouses were also established at ports and harbours, and the ports in north-west England, such as Morecambe and Heysham, and on the Isle of Man, such as Douglas, had their own aids to navigation, some of which were of notable size.

The Isle of Man

Lighthouse provision on the Isle of Man is somewhat unusual. At the start of the nineteenth century no major lights had been built on the island, and it was outside the jurisdiction of both Trinity House and the Commissioners of the Northern Lighthouses (NLB), the organisation responsible for lighthouses in Scotland. The NLB had been established in Edinburgh in 1786 by Act of Parliament, and authorised to build four lighthouses, with the first at Kinnaird Head, on Scotland's north-east coast, showing a light in 1787. The other early stations were

▲ The lighthouse at St Bees is one of the oldest on the Cumbrian coast.

◄ The Northern Lighthouse Board crest above the doorway of the shore building at Port St Mary.

Lighthouse History

▲ Douglas Head lighthouse on the Isle of Man came under the control of the Commissioners for Northern Lighthouses in August 1858 and is one of seven aids to navigation maintained by the Board on the island.

established at North Ronaldsay (Orkney), Scalpay (Outer Hebrides) and the Mull of Kintyre on the Kintyre peninsula.

The situation in Scotland was thus rather more straightforward than in England and Wales, with the Northern Lighthouse Board taking responsibility for the provision of aids to navigation more or less from the outset, as only a few private lights had been built. In 1801, following a visit to Man by its engineer Robert Stevenson, the Board investigated the possibility of erecting lighthouses on the island. Stevenson was concerned that the Manx coastline should be marked by a major lighthouse as soon as practicable, and investigated possible sites.

The Commissioners decided that two lighthouses should be erected, and the necessary power was procured by an Act of Parliament passed in 1815. Although Trinity House initially

objected to the plans, believing it was their chartered right to erect lighthouses on Man, the Northern Lighthouse Board was given jurisdiction over the Manx coastline and soon began work on the two new lights, one at the Point of Ayre in the north and a pair of lights at the Calf of Man, an island off Man's southern tip.

Over the next century further lighthouses were built by the Northern Lighthouse Board on the Isle of Man, with aids to navigation at Douglas Head, Chicken Rock, Maughold Head and Langness all becoming operational. Today, the Board is responsible for seven lighthouses on Man ranging from Point of Ayre and the Winkie in the north to the treacherous Chicken Rock in the south, all of which are automated. The last of the IOM lights to be automated was that at Langness in 1996. Local attendants are now responsible for managing the lights. The Manx lights are also visited regularly for storing and maintenance by the Board's ships, Pharos and Pole Star.

Harbour lights

Much of the literature about lighthouses has concentrated on the major lights, which are often impressive structures in spectacular locations. However, no less important are the many smaller lights found at most ports and harbours. These have developed in response to specific local circumstances, so their design, construction and purpose differ markedly and the variety of such lights is considerable.

Many harbour authorities are responsible for their own aids to navigation, and this has led to a variety of lights and beacons being erected. Some ports, where vessels need to follow channels, have leading or range lights which, when aligned, mark a safe passage. Others have long piers or breakwaters, the limits of which need marking, and on these some of the finest light towers have been constructed. The channels into the Mersey used by vessels destined for Liverpool were marked by a series of lights, some of which were shown from notable

▲ Maughold Head lighthouse on the east coast of the Isle of Man. This old photo shows the station when the fog horn was still in operation. The station was automated in 1993.

◄ Hale Head lighthouse on the north bank of the river Mersey. This tower was built in 1906 and used until 1958.

HALEHEAD LIGHTHOUSE.

Lighthouse History

▲ Langness lighthouse on the Isle of Man had quite extensive accommodation for the keepers, but since automation this has been sold and converted into private dwellings.

towers, but none of which remain operational today.

At other ports in the north-west where significant amounts of trade were handled, such as at Maryport and Whitehaven, new harbours were built with lighthouses to mark their entrances. On the Isle of Man, the local harbour lights, of which there are many, are managed and maintained by the Harbours Division of the island's government. Many of the smaller Manx lights are similar in appearance, and even the smallest ports on the island have aids to navigation.

Lightkeepers

Throughout the history of lighthouses, the lightkeeper has played an essential role in maintaining the light. However, during the latter half of the twentieth century, the era of manned lighthouses came to an end as automation took over,

and the keepers were withdrawn from all the major lighthouses. But before automation, every light had to be manned.

The idealised notion of lighthouse keepers conjures up a romantic image of men living in a tower with only the sea for company. While this was accurate for the rock stations, such as Chicken Rock, where keepers were confined to fairly cramped quarters for weeks at a time, the reality for most keepers was a little different.

Most major lights had a senior keeper supported by two assistant keepers, usually with their families. They would live in purpose-built accommodation adjacent to the lighthouse. Ensuring the light was working properly was a routine task. Since the lights have been automated, they are controlled from a central location with a local attendant responsible for minor maintenance work.

North West lighthouses

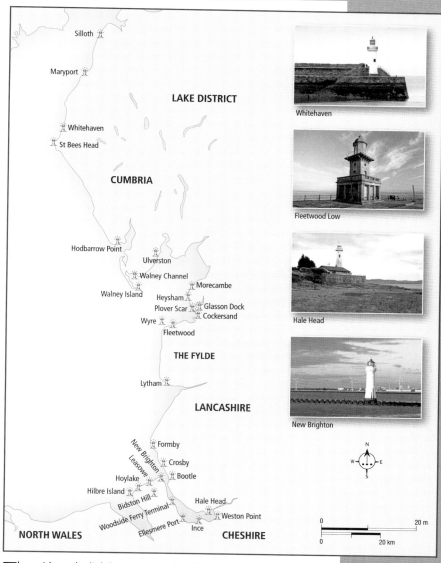

Silloth

Maryport

LAKE DISTRICT

Whitehaven
St Bees Head

CUMBRIA

Hodbarrow Point
Ulverston
Walney Channel
Walney Island
Morecambe
Heysham
Plover Scar
Glasson Dock
Cockersand
Wyre
Fleetwood

THE FYLDE

Lytham

LANCASHIRE

Formby
New Brighton
Leasowe
Crosby
Hoylake
Bootle
Hilbre Island
Bidston Hill
Woodside Ferry Terminal
Hale Head
Ellesmere Port
Ince
Weston Point

NORTH WALES

CHESHIRE

Whitehaven

Fleetwood Low

Hale Head

New Brighton

0   20 m
0   20 km

The guide to the lighthouses starts on the Wirral on the coast of Merseyside and traces the lights northwards to Lancashire and Cumbria, and then across to the Isle of Man. The photographs show the lighthouses as they are today. The information about visiting the lighthouses is only a starting point, and published road maps and Ordnance Survey maps should be used when going to any of the places mentioned.

See page 63 for Isle of Man map.

Hilbre Island

ESTABLISHED
1927

CURRENT TOWER
Prior to 1948

AUTOMATED
1927

OPERATOR
Trinity House

ACCESS
The island can be visited with care at low tide by walking across the sands from West Kirby; tide times and suitable visiting hours are on display at West Kirby

▼ The small light on Hilbre is at the end of the island furthest from the mainland.

Hilbre Island, now owned by Wirral Borough Council, is the largest of three islands to the east of the mouth of the Dee Estuary off Hoylake. The islands, composed of Bunter Sandstone, not only form a site of special scientific interest, but are also in the top ten European wading bird sanctuaries. Although only one person lives at Hilbre today, the island was occupied as early as Roman times.

For ten years from 1232 John Scott, the Earl of Chester, contributed ten shillings per year to the monks who lived there to provide lights on the island. However, it is not clear whether the lights were actually used for navigational purposes. Several centuries later, in 1813 two beacons were erected on the north side of the island to guide vessels through the Hilbre Swash, a channel between Hoylake sands and the Dee.

In 1828 the Trustees of Liverpool Docks obtained a lease on the island and in 1856 bought the island, having established a telegraph signalling station there in 1841. In 1927 they erected a navigation light, which forms a port landmark for the Swash. Situated at the north of the island, the light was originally a 10ft metal lattice tower but today it is smaller and shown from an enclosed metal box with solar panels mounted on top.

The light, originally acetylene powered, was transferred from Mersey Docks and Harbour Board to Trinity House in 1973 and in 1995 was converted to solar power. The red flashing light is visible for five miles. The future of lights in the Dee Estuary, including Hilbre, is currently under review and the future for this light is uncertain.

Hoylake

The town of Hoylake takes its name from the large pool, called Hoyle Lake, in which ships moored to offload heavier cargo prior to sailing up the rivers Mersey or Dee. This cargo was transported by road to Chester or Liverpool where the lighter cargo was landed by ship. Thus, when two lighthouses were built by the Mersey Harbour Authority in 1764, they became known locally as the Lake Lights.

The lower or front light, originally a wooden structure about 25ft high, was situated on the shoreline and could be moved backwards or forwards to take into account shifting sands and tides. It was destroyed by sea erosion in 1771, but was rebuilt on a site adjacent to the lifeboat station in the late 1770s or early 1780s as a 42ft hexagonal castellated brick structure from which a light with a range of eleven miles was displayed. This light was deactivated in 1908 and in 1909 was sold to Charles Bertie Burrows for £936. It was demolished in 1922.

The higher or rear light was situated 500 yards inland, to the north-east, in Valencia Road. The original 55ft brick tower was replaced in 1864 by the present 72ft octagonal brick tower with attached buildings. The tower had accommodation for two families on four floors, as the lighthouse keepers were responsible for both lights. The light, visible for nine miles, was extinguished in May 1886, and the tower was sold to Captain Edward Cole Wheeler for £800 in 1909. Although land

between the lighthouses was purchased to avoid buildings obstructing the light, since 1886 development has taken place.

The lighthouse is now a private dwelling and, although the original optic is no longer in the tower, it is displayed on the ground floor of the attached house. Both lights were originally coal-fired, but were later converted to use Hutchinson's catoptric reflectors. The high light was the first lighthouse in the world to be so equipped, in 1772. The lighthouse structure in Stanley Road is a replica.

ESTABLISHED	
1764	
CURRENT TOWER	
1864	
DISCONTINUED	
1886	
OPERATOR	
Mersey Docks and Harbour Board	
ACCESS	
The old high light is 500 yards inland on private land at Valencia Road	

▼ The old high lighthouse at Hoylake is now a private house.

15

Bidston Hill

ESTABLISHED
1771

CURRENT TOWER
1873

DISCONTINUED
1913

ACCESS
East of M53 junction 1, on Eleanor Road, which is at junction of Worcester Road and Boundary Road

The Bidston Hill lighthouse was built on a hill some distance inland to mark the Lake channel and worked in conjunction with Hoylake high light after the low light was destroyed in 1771. The light, which was shown from a 55ft octagonal tower, was first lit in 1777. This tower was demolished in 1872 but replaced the following year by the present 69ft stone tower, and adjacent dwellings were constructed by the Mersey Docks and Harbour Board. The lighthouse was part of a complex which housed a signal station; semaphore signals could be sent between Holyhead and Bidston to warn if an enemy was approaching. This system enabled messages to be sent between Holyhead and Liverpool in just eight minutes.

In 1858 the service was superseded by the electric telegraph, and the lighthouse and telegraph services were amalgamated. An observatory was opened on the site in 1866. The lighthouse was deactivated in 1913 and, although the tower and observatory were subsequently restored and at one time opened as a museum, the buildings became disused with the closure of the complex.

▲ The inscription and date stone above the door of the old lighthouse at Bidston.

▶ The now disused lighthouse at Bidston Hill can be seen from main roads around the immediate area.

16

In 1763 two lighthouses were erected at Leasowe by Liverpool Council's Corporation Docks Committee (forerunner to the Mersey Docks and Harbour Board). When aligned, they marked the entry into the Rock Channel and then into Liverpool docks. The low light, situated a quarter of a mile out to sea, was destroyed by coastal erosion in 1769, so in 1771 a replacement was built on Bidston Hill, some distance behind the Leasowe light. The Leasowe high light became the front or low light, and the alignment with the light on Bidston Hill provided a safe approach to the Mersey.

The higher Leasowe light was a 110ft white-painted structure with a range of fifteen miles, built with 660,000 hand-made bricks and was the first brick-built tower lighthouse in Britain. Because the land on Leasowe Common is very boggy, the lighthouse was built on bales of cotton, which had been recovered from a shipwreck.

The light was originally coal fired, which meant that the coal had to be carried up seven floors via 149 cast iron stairs, something of a time-consuming operation. However, in 1772 the fire was replaced by a catoptric lantern with three burners, which proved a better arrangement. These lights were two of the four lights on the Wirral coast which marked the safe passage into Liverpool through the Horse Channel and into the river Mersey; the others were the pair of lights at Hoylake.

The light from the rear tower was discontinued on 5 July 1908, after which the Harbour Board substituted a system of red flashing buoys to mark the channel into the river, and the lighthouse became derelict.

However, this unusual and historic lighthouse was refurbished during the 1990s by the Friends of Leasowe Lighthouse, together with the support of Wirral Borough Council, and it remains standing in good condition. As well as housing a ranger service, the lighthouse is open to visitors every other Sunday afternoon from April to September.

ESTABLISHED
1763

CURRENT TOWER
1763

DISCONTINUED
1908

ACCESS
On the seafront west of Wallasey, the tower is open and access to the top is possible

▼ The historic eighteenth century lighthouse at Leasowe was restored during the 1990s, with the work completed in 1996.

New Brighton

▶▶ The elegant
lighthouse at New
Brighton is a major
landmark at the
entrance to the
river Mersey.

▼ The lighthouse
seen form the sea,
looking towards
Perch Fort, which
itself is open to
the public.

The lighthouse at New Brighton, known as Rock Light, marks the western side of the entrance to the river Mersey. A light was first erected here by Liverpool Corporation in 1683 because of the proximity of the Black Rock to the North Channel, where the Mersey opens out into Liverpool Bay. The light was originally mounted on a wooden 'perch' and the rock was renamed Perch Rock.

When foreign ships passed the light they were charged six pence for its upkeep, but the relatively weak structure was often washed away. In February 1821 the pilot boat Liver crashed into the perch and carried it away. By the 1820s, it was realised that the cost of replacing the light was too expensive and so a stronger tower was built.

The foundation stone of the new lighthouse was laid on 8 June 1827 by Thomas Littledale, Mayor of Liverpool. The tower was designed along the lines of the Eddystone tower by a Mr Foster and built of marble rock from Anglesey by Tomkinson & Company. The 90ft conical granite tower was completed in 1830 at a cost of £27,000, and first displayed a light on 1 March 1830. It later became known as the Perch Rock lighthouse.

The lower unpainted section of the tower was solid, while the upper section housed the keepers. Access was via a vertical ladder, which does not reach to ground level. The light was originally fixed white, but in 1878 was altered to flashing white. Eventually electrically lit, the revolving light, housed in a red-painted lantern room and visible for fourteen miles, was extinguished in October 1973, after which the lighthouse went into private ownership. The light is now used as a Morse code station, although messages are sent out only by request.

Woodside Ferry Terminal

ESTABLISHED
1840

CURRENT TOWER
1986 (replica)

DISCONTINUED
1855

ACCESS
The replica is on
the landing stage
of the Woodside
Ferry terminal at
Birkenhead

▶▶ The non-operational light
on the west bank
of the Mersey.

▼ The lighthouse
overlooks Woodside
Ferry Terminal and
the river Mersey.

A light was established at Woodside Ferry Terminal on the west bank of the Mersey, where the Liverpool-Birkenhead ferry crosses the river when a stone jetty was first erected in about 1840. The light was shown from a white lantern mounted on top of a conical white stone tower. The light was displayed through a window facing across the river.

Because of land reclamation, the light was lit for only about fifteen years or so, but surprisingly the tower remained for a further 140 years despite several substantial alterations to the terminal itself and the adjacent land. Photographs taken just before a major redevelopment of the area in the 1980s show the lantern atop a metal framework mounted on a square metal compartment, with a large bell suspended just beneath the lantern. The original concrete tower was also pictured minus the lantern.

When a completely new landing stage and terminal buildings were erected during 1985 and 1986, the original concrete tower was refurbished and the lantern replaced on top. Today, the non-operational tower, which is situated adjacent to the terminal building and close to now disused docks, is painted white and the lantern is a distinctive dark red. The bell, with its original metal housing, was restored and is now situated on the new landing stage.

Ellesmere Port

ESTABLISHED
1880

CURRENT TOWER
1880

DISCONTINUED
1894

ACCESS
The tower and
associated buildings
are part of the
Ellesmere Port Boat
Museum; the Museum
is open daily April
to October and
weekends in winter

▼ The lighthouse,
which originally
marked the entrance
locks to the
Shropshire Union
Canal, on South Pier
Road at Ellesmere
Port overlooking
the Manchester
Ship Canal.

WHITBY • As part of a project to connect the rivers Mersey, Dee and Severn, William Jessop built a canal from the Mersey at Netherpool to Ellesmere and Chester which opened in 1795. The section to the Severn was only partially completed. It was initially known as the Ellesmere Canal, but is now the Shropshire Union Canal

A dock complex called Whitby Docks was constructed at its junction with the Mersey in 1796 by Thomas Telford. This area now forms part of the town of Ellesmere Port, so named because it was the terminus of the canal from Ellesmere in Shropshire. At the docks goods brought by canal barge and rail were transferred to sea-going vessels.

To assist entry to the docks a 36ft octagonal red brick lighthouse, with adjoining buildings, was erected at its entrance in 1880 by J. Webb. This light, with its bell-shaped roof, was called Whitby lighthouse or sometimes Ellesmere Port lighthouse and was visible for nineteen miles. When the Manchester Ship Canal was built across the entrance in 1894, ships entered the docks via the Ship Canal, so the light became redundant and was discontinued.

In 1971 the Boat Museum Society opened the Boat Museum in the docks and the lighthouse became part of the National Waterways Museum. The lighthouse, which stands the museum grounds, has been restored and refurbished.

INCE • Between Ellesmere Port and Runcorn, on the south side of the Mersey, another light was built to mark Ince Bank. This was constructed in 1838, but was demolished in June 1865 and replaced by a new light, which itself ceased operation in 1877.

Just before Runcorn, at Weston Point, the river Mersey swings north and another river, the Weaver, enters on the southern shore. Before Hale Head light had been built on the north shore, a lighthouse was proposed to mark this point. Although mentioned as early as 1796, a light was not shown until 1810. However, the exact location or details of this early light are unknown. It was likely to have been on the island in a position similar to the second light, and was extinguished prior to 1843.

In 1843 a 30ft red circular sandstone lighthouse was built for the Weaver Navigation Co on the small island where the river Weaver joined the Mersey. It stood on a broad circular sandstone plinth and had three levels beneath a metal gallery, which had a hooded lantern and a domed roof. The light, shown through a window, faced the Mersey. In 1847 a bell was added to the tower and reflectors were fitted to the lantern.

When the Manchester Ship Canal was constructed in 1894 by the merchants of Manchester, so that they could avoid using Liverpool to move their products, the Canal crossed the river Weaver south of the lighthouse and greatly reduced the use of the river. The entry to the Weaver moved from the Mersey to the Ship Canal, and as a consequence the lighthouse became redundant and was deactivated in 1911.

As a result, the lighthouse became isolated and both it and the nearby Christ Church fell into disrepair. By the 1930s the lantern had been removed and in 1960 the lighthouse was demolished. The remains of the church are still visible from the canal, giving a rough indication of the lighthouse's location, but nothing remains of the tower.

ESTABLISHED
1810

SECOND TOWER
1843

OPERATOR
Weaver Navigation Company

DEACTIVATED
1911, demolished 1960

▼ The 1843 lighthouse at Weston Point, on the junction of the rivers Weaver and Mersey, was demolished in 1960.

Hale Head

ESTABLISHED
1838

CURRENT TOWER
1906

DISCONTINUED
1958

ACCESS
Hale Head can be
reached on foot
from Hale Church via
Lighthouse Road; the
Mersey Way Coast
Path also passes
nearby

▶▶ The lighthouse
at Hale Head dates
from 1906, and was
operated until 1958.

▼ The lighthouse
of 1838 was
demolished in 1906
but the keepers'
cottage was used
as part of the
new tower.

Situated on the north bank of the river Mersey, where the river bends between Liverpool and Runcorn, the head at Hale juts out and is an important landmark for shipping. To provide guidance, in 1838 a lighthouse was built there, consisting of a squat hexagonal 18ft tower, complete with gallery and lantern. Attached to it via a corridor was the keeper's cottage.

This lighthouse was demolished in 1906, when a new tower was built a few feet away. Alongside the original building, an extended keepers' dwelling was constructed, and this was connected to the new tower by a short corridor.

The new lighthouse was 58ft in height with the circular, slightly tapered brick tower supporting a gallery and lantern. It was attached to the adjacent keeper's cottage by a corridor. When the light was operational, a fog bell was attached to the gallery and a weather vane was placed on the metal roof, with a flag pole attached to the lantern. The oil-powered fixed white light was visible for six miles.

During a Second World War air raid, the keeper was fired on as she tried to close the shutters. In 1958 the light was extinguished, initially on a trial basis, but it was never relit and the lighthouse was deactivated. The tower of the 1906 lighthouse is now a grade II listed building, but the keepers' cottages have been replaced by a modern residence.

The light mechanism and fog bell have been removed from the lantern and are on display at the Merseyside Maritime Museum in Albert Dock, Liverpool. When operational, the lighthouse was directly on the foreshore, but since then a substantial seawall to prevent erosion has been constructed around the area.

Hale Lighthouse, near Liverpool. No. 13.

River Mersey

BOOTLE

ESTABLISHED
1877

DISCONTINUED
1927

OPERATOR
Mersey Docks and
Harbour Board

The port of Liverpool, with its associated dock system, is one of the country's busiest ports and the river Mersey has long been an important shipping channel. The old lighthouses at Formby, Crosby and Bootle, none of which now exist, at one time marked the approaches to this busy river.

FORMBY • The northern approach to the river Mersey is strewn with shifting sandbanks and channels so to aid shipping a pair of tapered circular white-painted brick towers was erected in 1719 in the sand dunes at Formby Point, about a mile from

the end of what is today Albert Road. The high tower was 120ft tall and the low tower 80ft. When in line they marked the channel between Madwharf and Burbo Bank.

In 1833 the Mersey Docks and Harbour Board converted the high tower into a lighthouse operating in conjunction with the Formby lightvessel. First lit on 1 August 1834, it showed a yellow light visible for twelve miles. On 1 February 1838 it was altered to fixed red but was discontinued on 10 October 1839 after the channel had changed. It was resurrected for a time, from 16 October 1851 to 6 October 1856, but was then permanently extinguished. The tower was demolished by the War Office in August 1941.

CROSBY • When the channel altered and the light at Formby was discontinued, it was replaced by Crosby lighthouse, which was some distance north of Crosby village near Hightown. The first lighthouse, built in 1839, was a 96ft slender wooden tower supported with wooden outriggers in the sand dunes not far from the railway station. Erected by the Liverpool Dock Authority and first lit on 10 October 1839, it showed a fixed red light visible for sixteen miles. It was not a success, due to the ever-changing channels in the area, and was replaced just eight years after being built by another, half-a-mile to the north-east.

Built by the newly-formed Mersey Docks and Harbour Board

▼ The 1719 high lighthouse at Formby, which was demolished by the War Office in 1941.

and designed by the Board's chief engineer Jesse Hartley, this light was of a much more substantial construction, consisting of a 74ft tapering square brick tower with an iron gallery on which stood a wooden lantern, making the whole structure 95ft in height. An attached keepers' dwelling was, like the tower, painted white. The fixed white light, visible for twelve miles, was displayed from 2 November 1847 until 16 October 1851 and then again from 6 October 1856.

On 2 February 1898 a fierce gale broke the lantern room windows causing burning oil from the light to fall onto the wooden floor. The lighthouse went up in flames and the keeper, his wife and a friend were killed. A temporary light was installed but the light was permanently extinguished in July. No sign of this light now exists and the much-changed coastline makes it impossible to identify its location.

BOOTLE • Looking at twenty-first century Bootle, it is difficult to visualise the scene in the nineteenth century, when Liverpool was just starting to encroach. The village had an extensive sea frontage, and to assist ships entering the expanding docks, a lighthouse was erected on the North Wall near the lock gates to Hornby Dock. Built in 1877 by the Mersey Docks and Harbour Board, it was an ornate square two-storey red brick building. The substantial gallery supported a large lantern which had a domed roof, bringing

the height to 75ft. To deflect the light seaward, the rear of the lantern was solid.

Known as North Wall Light, it showed a fixed white light visible for twelve miles, and was first lit on 1 October 1877. As the docks were further expanded, the light was extinguished, and in 1927 the tower was demolished when the new Gladstone Dock was constructed. During its operational days, it was known locally as the Bootle Bull because of its deep foghorn. Today, a simple 29ft white concrete post supports a navigation light to the north of the dock entrance.

FORMBY

ESTABLISHED
1719

CURRENT TOWER
1856

OPERATOR
Mersey Docks and Harbour Board

▼ The red brick lighthouse at Hornby Dock in 1877 was demolished in 1927 when Gladstone Dock was constructed.

Lytham

ESTABLISHED
1848

CURRENT TOWER
1988

OPERATOR
Ribble Cruising Club

ACCESS
The church is
on the front in
Fairhaven Road

▼ Engraving of the
stone lighthouse
built at Lytham
in 1848 which
collapsed into the
sea in January 1863.

The entry to the river Ribble has always been challenging, with a series of shifting sandbanks covering more than fifty square miles with navigable channels continually changing. To assist shipping a lighthouse, built in 1847 but not lit until 1 February 1848, was erected on a stone stanner to seaward of what is now Lightburne Avenue in Fairhaven. Locally referred to as Lytham or Stanner Point light, it was a 72ft bell-bottomed circular brick tower with gallery and lantern. A fixed white light was shown and an additional fixed red light was displayed from a small gallery a third of the way down the tower. Encroachment by the sea undermined it, and on 22 January 1863 it completely collapsed into the sea.

In its place, a temporary pile light was established nearby. This was replaced in 1864 by a new 81ft octagonal wooden tower erected further inland, but still on the sand dunes. First lit on 1 January 1865, it showed two lights like its predecessor: one occulting white light from the lantern on top, with a fixed white tide light lower down. This second light was discontinued in 1890 when a gas-lit buoy

replaced the previously unlit Nelson Buoy in the river mouth. The structure decayed over time and was demolished in 1901.

In 1906 a third Lytham light was erected on a pile platform twelve and a quarter miles from Preston Docks, on the north bank of the Gut Channel. Known as Peet's light because Jack Peet worked on it, the structure was partially destroyed by fire in 1954, but a light was exhibited from it until 1985, when the piles themselves were washed away leaving no trace today.

In 1998 a Trinity House-approved light, belonging to Ribble Cruising Club, was placed on the tower of Fairhaven United Reformed Church to act as a leading light for the gap from

South Gut to the Gut Channel. It is mounted 33ft below the top of the 142ft church tower. Originally a flashing white light, it now shows an isophase white light, which is visible for three miles.

▲ The remains of the pile platform erected on the North Wall on the banks of the river Ribble just over twelve miles from Preston Docks.

◀ The timber lighthouse which stood on the dunes. It was first lit in January 1865, replacing a collapsed stone-built predecessor, and became a well-known landmark until its removal.

Fleetwood

ESTABLISHED
1840

CURRENT TOWER
1840

OPERATOR
Associated British
Ports

ACCESS
Both lights are easily
seen: the Low Light is
on the seafront and
the High Light is in
Pharos Road

▶▶ The low light
at Fleetwood
was designed by
Decimus Burton and
is as grand today as
when first built.

▼ The low light
on the promenade
overlooks the
entrance to
the Wyre.

In the early part of the nineteenth century Sir Peter Hesketh masterminded a plan to build a port and holiday resort on the land he owned, and the result was the town of Fleetwood. Although Hesketh went bankrupt before finishing it, his vision was more enacted. The architect Decimus Burton was commissioned to produce plans for the town, and, as well as the famous North Euston Hotel, he designed the two lighthouses, with the assistance of Captain H. M. Denham. The lights, one in the town and the other on the promenade, and the hotel are Burton's most famous buildings.

The lighthouses were designed to be used as a pair to guide shipping through the treacherous sandbanks of the Wyre estuary and into the port. The high light, known locally as the Pharos, consists of a 90ft red stone circular tower on a square stone base. Near the top is a stone gallery with metal railings and the light, shown through a narrow vertical window, came from a stone lantern with a domed roof. The green flashing light, visible for thirteen miles, guides vessels into the correct channel. Somewhat unusual for a functioning British lighthouse, it stands in the middle of a residential area in Pharos Street, 350 yards from the sea.

The low light consists of a square shelter with covered seating and gothic columns. The seating was provided for Victorian visitors who were 'promenading' along the harbour front. The roof has an ornate stone balustrade inside which is a second tier square tower topped with a balcony. The structure is completed by a hexagonal stone lantern with a domed roof.

Fleetwood

▶ The two lights at Fleetwood must be aligned for a safe passage in and out of the port.

▶▶ The tall high light is a notable landmark in the middle of the town.

▼ An old postcard of the high light with the low light visible to the left.

The 43ft tower displays a green flashing light visible for nine miles, shown through a window. Construction of the lights was completed in 1840.

For vessels using the port, the light from the Pharos is kept above the lower light to give a safe passage down the channel. Both lighthouses were first shown on the same day, 1 December 1840. The gas was supplied by the Fleetwood Gas Co, which also supplied gas for the lighting on the sea front. The lamp in the Upper light is 104ft above sea level, and the light has a range of twelve miles.

The lighthouse was painted cream and red, but in the late 1970s the paint was stripped off to expose the sandstone. Neither of the towers are open to the public. Fleetwood was once home to a significant fishing fleet, but the only significant vessels that use the port today are the ro-pax ferries to Ireland.

Wyre

▼ Wyre light, now derelict but pictured when in operation, stood on seven screw piles sunk into the seabed at the northern edge of North Wharf, the sandbank stretching from Fleetwood to the edge of Lune Deeps in Morecambe Bay.

As well as the high and low lighthouses at Fleetwood, a lighthouse was built to guard the entry into the pot in 1840. Situated just over a mile offshore, it marked the North Wharf Bank at the mouth of the Wyre, and was notable as only the second screw pile lighthouse in the world. The blind Irish engineer Alexander Mitchell designed the structure, which was the forerunner of screw pile lights round the world making it of considerable importance and its dilapidated condition regrettable.

The tower consisted of seven cast-iron legs screwed into the sandbank. Each leg was 16ft long and 3ft in diameter, and six were placed at an angle of one in five to form a hexagonal 50ft base, with one vertical leg in the centre. This supported an oval platform on which stood a single-storey wood and corrugated iron accommodation block. On the roof of this block stood a hexagonal lantern room with an iron roof topped by a weather vane. Its fixed white light was visible for ten miles and a boat was slung beneath from davits.

The whole structure was 40ft in height and was originally painted red. In 1870 the tower was rammed by the schooner Elizabeth and Jane, of Preston, after which it was re-erected and the colour changed to black to make it more conspicuous.

In 1948 the lighthouse was destroyed by fire and, although the three keepers were rescued by the Fleetwood lifeboat, the lighthouse itself was not replaced and fell into disrepair. A navigation light was displayed from the remains of the platform until 1979, when a navigation buoy was placed nearby and the light was extinguished, leaving a marvel of Victorian engineering to decay.

▲ The remains of the Wyre light at high tide.

◄ The remains of the Wyre light, pictured during the Fleetwood Lifeboat Annual Wreck Trek in June 2007. It is possible, at low tide, to walk out to the remains of this historic structure, and each year, for a small donation, people are escorted across the sands to see the tower.

Cockersand

ESTABLISHED
1847

TOWER BUILT
1847

DISCONTINUED
1985

ACCESS
The wooden tower was demolished in 1954 and only the keepers' cottage remains

In 1847 a pair of lighthouses was built to guide ships into the safe channel of the river Lune and onwards to Glasson Docks. The Rear Range light, sometimes called Cockersand high or upper lighthouse, was designed by John B. Hartley, Chief Engineer to the Mersey Docks and Harbour Board, and built by Charles Blades on land near Cockersand Abbey. It consisted of a 54ft shingle-covered square wooden tower steadied by two wooden props at each corner.

The square lantern above the gallery was also wooden, and had a pitched roof. Built within the corner stays were four identical keepers' quarters, but later a stone cottage with a slate roof was added and this building still exists. The fixed white light, which was displayed from a window in one side of the lantern, was visible for nine miles. Originally fuelled by two paraffin wick lamps and parabolic reflectors with candles as a back up, the light was converted to electricity in 1947.

In 1953 the light was replaced by a 54ft red-painted square steel tower with a pair of twelve-volt bulbs complete with a magnifier and reflector. They were initially switched on manually, but made automatic towards the end of the 1950s. The original wooden tower was demolished in 1954. By 1985 the need for the light had diminished so it was extinguished and the steel tower was demolished. Only the keepers' cottage remains, near Cockersand Abbey.

▼ The wooden lighthouse at Cockersand was demolished in 1954.

Of the 1847-built lighthouses to guide ships into river Lune, the Front Range was erected 400 yards out to sea on a reef called Plover Scar, after which it is named. It was designed and built by John B. Hartley. This unusual 58ft circular stone tower is tapered up to the lower gallery. The lower section is unpainted with the upper section painted white. Between the two galleries, the tower is of white-painted hexagonal stone, and above the second gallery the light is displayed from a circular lantern with a black domed roof complete with weather vane.

The light was originally paraffin fuelled but was converted to automatic solar power in 1951. The flashing white light is visible for seven miles.

For almost a century, from 1847 until 1945, members of the same family were keepers to both lights. Francis Raby commenced in 1847, followed by Henry Raby in the 1870s and finally Janet Raby and her brother Richard Raby who carried out the duties until the end of 1945. They were followed by the Parkinson family, Thomas and Beatrice Parkinson, and their son Richard.

ESTABLISHED
1847

CURRENT TOWER
1847

ACCESS
Although offshore, the tower can be seen from the beach and approached with care at low tide

◀ The lighthouse at Plover Scar was operated by a family of lighthouse keepers at one time. In 1948 one of the keepers, Mrs Beatrice Parkinson, obtained notoriety when she appeared in national magazines as the only female lighthouse keeper in Britain, a claim which is somewhat surprising as her husband was actually the keeper.

Glasson Dock

ESTABLISHED
1836

CURRENT TOWER
1836

ACCESS
Access to Glasson is permitted, but care needs to be taken as the light itself is in a working area

Glasson Dock, situated at the entrance to the river Lune, was built in 1787 as a port for the town of Lancaster because the shallowness of the river and a rock bar prevented many vessels from reaching the quays in the centre of the town. Although the port was only accessible for an hour each side of high water, it became one of the busiest in the country during the eighteenth century.

The entrance to the dock was marked in 1836 by a lantern mounted on the roof of a small watch house at the end of the dock wall. This lantern displayed a fixed white light with a range of two miles. The watch house was a white-painted stone building, and it is still standing. It had an apex tiled roof with the light displayed from a hexagonal lantern at one end. It became disused when new training walls and quays were built to enable a new deepwater channel to be dredged from Glasson to Lancaster and thus improve access to the port.

The building is now dwarfed by a warehouse within the port complex. The docks themselves have seen a revival not only as a working port handling a variety of cargoes, but also with a marina used by pleasure craft. The area's modern navigation lights are exhibited from a series of electric lights on a trellis tower behind the old watch house.

▼ The small disused lighthouse with its steeply-pointed dome lantern at Glasson Dock.

The creation of the port of Heysham came about as a result of the growth of traffic across the Irish Sea towards the end of the nineteenth century. The Midland Railway Company, which operated the railways in the area, realised that the port of Barrow was too far from the nearest large towns and Morecambe was not practical as a port as it dried out for many hours each day. This meant that the only deep water facilities were at the port of Fleetwood, but these were rather limited.

So the company decided to seek an Act of Parliament in 1896 to authorise the construction of a new port at Heysham, which would be connected to the inland population by a direct railway. The new port, which consisted of a harbour enclosed by two long breakwaters, was opened on 1 September 1904 when the steamships Antrim and Londonderry took company officials and employees across the Irish Sea to Douglas and Belfast. Once established, the port played a major role in developing trade links with Belfast and other Irish ports, and it now enjoys a busy trade. It effectively took over from Barrow, Morecambe and Fleetwood as the main English port for traffic to the Isle of Man and Ireland.

The port's builders had the foresight to provide the whole complex with electricity, making the port unique in its day. Today ferry services operate to Dublin, Belfast and Warrenpoint, and cargo and passenger sailings go to the Isle of Man. The port, currently owned by Peel Ports, is also a base for supply vessels to one of a large offshore gas field.

ESTABLISHED
1904

CURRENT TOWER
1904

OPERATOR
Associated British Ports

ACCESS
Both piers have public access, while good views of the lights can be had from the regular ferries that use the port

▼ The light at the end of Heysham South Pier.

Heysham

With the new port inevitably came new aids to navigation and, to help vessels avoid the rocky area known as Near Naze in Half Moon Bay, just outside the harbour entrance, a 30ft three-storey round stone tower, with a gallery was erected in 1904. It is not certain when, but certainly before 1916, this light was replaced by a 69ft cast iron skeleton tower, which was mounted on a circular stone base a short distance to seaward of the original tower off Shore Road, near Portway.

This second light, which operated as a rear range light with the South Pier light, has been deactivated and the skeleton tower removed. Today the stone base can be seen near the redundant 1904 tower, which remains virtually intact with the disused navigational light.

When the docks were constructed, another lighthouse was built on the end of the south pier. Mounted on a circular 20ft red-painted cast iron tower with gallery, it shows an occulting green light with the character six seconds on, one and a half seconds off. It is visible for six miles from a white lantern, which has a domed roof topped by a weather vane. It is known as Heysham Harbour South Pier Head, and it was operated as a front range with the Near Naze light during that light's existence. That light was known as Heysham North Pier Range Rear.

On the end of the south breakwater is a 20ft white post, which shows two fixed green lights, one above the other. Built in 1929, this is not to be confused with the 13ft circular tower with a gallery, just behind which is a building that looks like a lighthouse but is actually a fog signal, and which gives a blast every thirty seconds. Exposure has taken its toll on the breakwater, leaving the area around the light and fog signal somewhat isolated.

▶▶ The Near Naze light erected in 1904 had a short life, but the tower remains in good condition.

▼ An old postcard showing the lighthouse on the end of the south pier erected in 1904 when the docks were constructed.

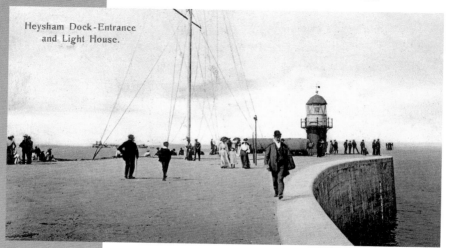

Heysham Dock - Entrance and Light House.

Morecambe

▶▶ Morecambe
light, overlooking
Morecambe Bay,
was built for the
railway ferries
sailing to Ireland.

▼ The lighthouse
is at the end of the
Stone Pier, attached
to the old railway
station, which is
now a café.

Morecambe was a busy port during the nineteenth century. The harbour was built at Morecambe in the 1850s because ever larger ships could not use Glasson Dock, the port for Lancaster so a new port was needed. The new harbour was partially formed by the Stone Jetty, which was completed in 1853 and reached out to the deepwater channel. A railway line joined it to the mainline railway and enabled Morecambe to became a major player in the export of coal to Ireland.

To guide ships towards the jetty, a 36ft octagonal stone lighthouse on a square plinth was built on the seaward side of the railway terminus building in 1815 to the design of Thomas Stevenson. Called Morecambe Stone Pier Head, it had a stone gallery with black railings

accessed via a ladder up the end wall of the railway building, with a gantry onto the gallery where a small door gave entry to the lantern, although this is no longer accessible. The flashing white light, visible for three miles, is displayed from a white octagonal lantern with an ornate copper roof. Today, weather measuring devices are attached to the top.

With the development of Heysham as a port, Morecambe declined as a harbour and the railway yard closed in 1932. However, at the end of the twentieth century, as part of a major redevelopment of the area to attract visitors, the jetty was refurbished and extended, and the lighthouse was retained as a feature. The light is still shown across the Bay from the 26ft tower, and its fixed white light has a range of three miles.

Walney Island

ESTABLISHED
1790

CURRENT TOWER
1804

OPERATOR
Lancaster Port
Commission

ACCESS
The nearest public
access is the nature
reserve, from where
it is a short walk to
the lighthouse

▶▶ Walney Island
lighthouse stands at
the southern tip of
the Island.

▼ The lighthouse
at Walney was
built in 1804
and is operated
by the local port
commissioners.

In the 1700s the main port in the Morecambe Bay area was Glasson Dock, and Barrow was just a small fishing village. So in 1790, when a lighthouse was built at Haws Point on Walney Island, its purpose was to guide ships using the river Lune and not the Walney Channel and Barrow Docks. It was built by Lancaster Port Commissioners, who still operate it today.

The first lighthouse was a wooden tower with an oil lamp with parabolic reflectors. To distinguish it from St Bees and the Mersey lights, a revolving apparatus built by Richard Walker was installed. A flashing light was produced by fixing three parabolic reflectors back to back on an axle driven by a weight which dropped down the tower.

In 1803 the whole structure burned to the ground, and so it was replaced the following year by the 80ft octagonal tower which survives today. The stone for both the tower and attached keepers' dwelling was quarried in Overton in Lancashire and brought to the site by ship. The dwellings were originally one, but were later split into two properties. An Argand lamp was used until 1909 when an acetylene-powered flashing light system was installed.

In 1953 the station was converted to electrical operation with a generator, and it was connected to mains electricity in 1969. The weight-driven motor, which powered the rotating mechanism, was replaced by an electrical one in 1956. The station has what is reputed to be the last catoptric apparatus in England. The current light is visible for eighteen miles. The reflectors from the original apparatus are displayed at Lancaster Museum.

Walney Channel

Barrow-in-Furness, the major port between Liverpool and Glasgow, is best known for its long shipbuilding tradition. Entry to the port is via the Walney and Piel Channels, which require careful navigation, and a series of aids to navigation have been erected to assist vessels negotiating them. Training walls have been built in the approach to the docks, but beyond them the channel passes between Roa Island, Piel Island and the Piel Bar off the south east of Walney Island.

Although there is a lighthouse at the tip of Walney Island, its main purpose is to guide vessels into Lancaster, not up the channels into Barrow. Consequently a series of thirteen range lights was built between 1850 and 1870 to guide vessels into the port, only one of which survives today. Built of brick, this 46ft narrow square brick tower, with a pyramidal top, is situated on marshland to the side of the main road through Rampside. The bricks are red on the corners and yellowish white in the centre, giving the impression of a band on each side. The isophase white light, visible for six miles, is displayed from a window near the top. As a result of pressure from local inhabitants, this light, which is known locally as 'The Needle', is now a listed structure.

The original front light has been replaced by a modern glass-reinforced plastic tower on the shingle bank leading to Foulney Island from the road to Roa Island. Also known as Foulney Island Light, it consists of a 36ft prefabricated circular tower tapered at the bottom and top with, above the solar panels, a simple quick-flashing white navigation light visible for ten miles. In common with all the pile lights, it is managed by Associated British Ports.

Although the old brick lights have been demolished, they have been replaced by a series of range lights. One pair is situated at Biggar Sands on the west side of the channel, another pair at Rampside Sands and a third

►► The tall brick lighthouse at Rampside, known as Walney Channel Middle Range Rear, is the only remaining one of nine towers built between 1850 and 1870 marking the Walney Channel.

► The light tower on Foulness Island replace a structure similar to the one at Rampside.

Walney Channel

pair at the entrance to Walney Channel. They consist of pile structures with a variety of light configurations. In addition, a pair of pile lights is situated at Haws Point on the southern tip of Walney Island.

The Walney Channel between the training walls is marked by a series of simple pole lights. These are at Pike Stones Bed, at the elbow, and pile lights in the channel called Walney Channel East and West. In addition, a pair of pile lights marks the entrance channel into Ramsden Dock and lights are displayed at the dock entrance itself. It is possible

to view the channel lights by travelling Cistercian Way down Walney Island, with the pile lights Head Scar and Pickle Scar being the most noteworthy.

ULVERSTON • The Sir John Barrow Monument in Ulverston, which looks like a lighthouse on the summit of Hoad Hill east of the town, can be seen from the A590. Its lighthouse appearance is not surprising as, when built by public subscription in 1850, Trinity House donated £100 towards the £1,250 costs on the basis that it could be used as a lighthouse if required.

Situated approximately a mile from Morecambe Bay, the 100ft monument is built from limestone quarried at Birkrigg Common. It is modelled on the famous Eddystone lighthouse, a traditional rock lighthouse, and has a profile tapering more steeply at the base. The internal spiral staircase consists of 112 narrow steps leading to a lantern chamber, which has never had a functional light.

The somewhat ornate lantern room, complete with a pepper pot roof, was originally open on all sides, but to protect the tower it is now fully glazed. Subsequent deterioration led to it being encased in reinforced cement in 1969. It has been open to the public at various times, but since 2003 it has been closed as repairs are needed. An application for lottery funding has been made so that it can be reopened. On top of a 440ft hill, it can be reached via local footpaths.

Hodbarrow Point

ESTABLISHED
1866

CURRENT TOWER
1905

DISCONTINUED
1949, recommissioned 2003

OPERATOR
Local committee

ACCESS
On the sea wall, reached from the Haverigg end; the old light can be seen from the new light

The lighthouses at Hodbarrow Point have also been known as Haverigg, Hodbarrow Seawall or Millom Breakwater Light, and date from 1866, when the Hodbarrow Mining Company built a 35ft circular stone tower lighthouse at Rock House to aid shipping using the company's jetties to load iron ore. Situated at what was then the extremity of the mine workings, it had a gallery with the fixed white light shown through a small circular window on the seaward side.

Between 1900 and 1905, because its workings extended under Duddon Estuary, the Mining Company built a sea wall across part of the estuary and, as the lighthouse was then some distance inland, it was deactivated on 15 July 1905.

In the same year, a new light was erected on a 30ft two-storey cast-iron tower complete with gallery and lantern in the centre of the newly-completed sea wall. The lower cast-iron section was manufactured by Cochran & Son whilst the lantern, with domed roof and weather vane,

was made by Barbier, Bernard & Turenne of Paris. The lamp probably used a Fresnel lens with a revolving shutter mechanism, giving a white occulting light. The light, fuelled by paraffin, was visible for twelve miles.

By 1949 the mine's output had declined and the jetties were unsafe, so the company closed the mine and deactivated the light. Both towers then gradually deteriorated until, in 2003, a local school initiative, funded by a £20,000 lottery grant, saw the seawall light restored, and it was painted white with red trim.

Although efforts were made to restore the lighthouse to the original specification, the original internal arrangements, such as the supports for the fog bell, could not be replicated and so were omitted. The lantern, which originally had curved glass panes, now has flat sheets of glass held by additional supports. A new navigation lantern was installed to give a white flashing light visible for two miles which has been displayed during the hours of darkness since 2003.

►► The restored lighthouse at Hodbarrow Point is now fitted with a Carmanah solar-powered lantern which has displayed a light since 11 November 2003.

► The remains of the 1866-built stone lighthouse have been left untouched and open to the elements. The towers are situated within an RSPB nature reserve, which was created when the mine was flooded.

St Bees Head

ESTABLISHED
1718

CURRENT TOWER
1866

AUTOMATED
1987

OPERATOR
Trinity House

ACCESS
From St Bees village
via a mile walk along
the cliff path or from
a private car park at
North Head

▶▶ The buildings
at St Bees date
from 1866, and a
fog horn is situated
to seaward of
the station.

▼ The lighthouse
at St Bees stands
340ft above mean
sea level and is thus
the highest light in
England and Wales.

In north-west England, between the Welsh and Scottish borders, the only headland is that at North Head, a mile north of the small village of St Bees. As it represents a danger to shipping trading between the ports of Wales and those in the Solway Firth, such as Maryport, Workington, Whitehaven and Silloth, in 1718 Trinity House gave Thomas Lutwige a licence to build a 30ft coal-fired light or beacon on the headland. This was financed from dues of three-half pence a ton levied on cargo carried by vessels calling at the Cumbrian ports.

The lease was granted for ninety-nine years at an annual rent of £20. Lutwige had built a round tower, 30ft in height and 16ft in diameter, of local sandstone, with a large metal grate on top into which the keepers tipped coal. The small grate led to complaints from shipowners that, on windy nights, the light was variable in intensity and often shrouded in smoke.

In 1822 Lutwige's tower was destroyed by fire and so Trinity House replaced it in the same year, at a cost of £2,322, with a white-painted 55ft circular brick-built tower with attached dwellings to the design of Joseph Nelson that stands today. The new tower was fitted with oil-powered Argand lamps and reflectors. In 1866 Nelson's tower was superseded by a new lighthouse with attached dwellings, further inland, built under the supervision of James Douglas, and fitted with a large optic giving an occulting light.

Because of the height of the cliffs, the light is 340ft above mean sea level, even though the tower is relatively short. The light rotates with a white flashing light and is visible for over twenty miles. The station was automated and demanned in 1987.

Whitehaven

ESTABLISHED
1742

CURRENT TOWER
1841

OPERATOR
Whitehaven Harbour

ACCESS
All the lights can be
viewed by walking the
various harbour piers

▶▶ Reputedly the
earliest lighthouse
at Whitehaven, on
the Old Outer Quay,
was constructed
in 1742 but made
redundant by the
outer harbour lights.

▼ The building on
the Old Quay, used
as a watchtower,
may also have
displayed a light
when the pier on
which it stands was
the outermost quay.

The docks at Whitehaven were
developed over a period
of 300 years from the mid-
seventeenth century. The port is
the oldest on the Cumbrian coast,
having been created in 1690 by
Sir John Lowther, and developed
later by John Smeaton. The trade
in coal was superseded by iron
ore and then chemicals and as a
result the port has several jetties.

The oldest of the lighthouses
still in existence is that on
the Old Outer Quay. This was
erected in 1742 and consisted
of a 46ft three-storey circular
stone tower with gallery. The
light was displayed through a
window. A redundant two-storey
stone building, with a slate
roof adjacent to the tower, was
possibly associated with the
lighthouse. Fired by oil and from
1841 by gas, the light was made
redundant when the two lights in
the outer harbour were built, but
the tower remains a landmark.

Another tall circular stone
tower with an adjacent stone
two-storey building and slate
roof is located on the knuckle
of the Old Quay. This quay was
constructed in three stages –
1634, 1665 and 1687 – and the
tower on the then terminus built
sometime before 1730. Although
it is thought that this tower was
used solely as a watchtower, the
round railings on the top may be
the remains of a fire grate. As it
was built on what was at one
time the outermost quay, some
form of warning light would have
been displayed.

This tower has been
restored and the windows near
the top, which face seaward,
are a recent addition, although
a window did exist before. The
Old Quay was further extended
in 1809. In 2000 gates were
erected between the Old Quay
and Old North Wall to enclose a
new marina area.

Whitehaven

In 1841 a new pier was constructed to the north of the harbour entrance, and a conical brick tower, the North Pier Light, erected on its end. This 20ft white-painted tower, castellated with a gallery halfway up, displayed a fixed red light visible for nine miles through a window. Today two red lights are displayed, one above the other, on a mast atop the tower.

A second pier extending out from the Old New Quay, known as the West Pier, was constructed between 1824 and 1838. On its end, a 47ft tapered conical brick lighthouse, complete with gallery and lantern room, was erected. Its exact date of construction was probably 1841. This tower, now painted white with a red trim to the base and red gallery railings, carries a green flashing light which is visible for thirteen miles and housed in a lantern room with an ornate domed roof. The two active lighthouses were painted in 1999 and action is being taken to restore them.

▶▶ The light on the West Pier of Whitehaven harbour was built in the mid-nineteenth century and is the tallest of the town's lights.

▶ The tower on Whitehaven's North Pier displays two red lights, with its build date indicated.

Maryport

ESTABLISHED
circa 1796

CURRENT TOWER
1996

OPERATOR
Trinity House

ACCESS
Both lights can be viewed by walking the southern outer piers of the harbour

▶▶ The old lighthouse is a distinctive landmark at the harbour entrance.

▶ The current operational light is maintained by Trinity House, dates from the 1990s and has a range of six miles.

▼ The two lights at Maryport with the cast-iron lighthouse on the right.

Development of the port of Maryport began in 1749 when Humphrey Senhouse II began work on new quays to enable coal to be exported, and he named the town after his wife Mary. The first lighthouse for the port was erected on the end of the south pier in about 1796. George Stephenson reported, during his 1801 tour, that the light was fired by oil and employed two reflectors.

In 1846 this light was replaced by a cast-iron tower with a lantern on top, mounted on a stone polygon base. The light was visible for twelve miles. It was converted to acetylene in 1946 and, although taken over by Trinity House in 1961, was powered by acetylene until 1996, when it was replaced by a rather bland triangular aluminium tower, which has an electrically-powered navigation light mounted on its seaward side.

The exact date of the light's decommissioning may have been earlier, as Trinity House erected a light on a short concrete column prior to the construction of the aluminium tower. The 1846 light still exists and is reputedly the oldest cast-iron lighthouse in existence. It is an unusual design, with the black-painted lantern supported by a narrow white cast iron column on a broad base. The structure is mounted on a 6ft hexagonal base. Maryport has been redeveloped for visitors, and both lights are accessible.

Silloth

ESTABLISHED
1841

CURRENT TOWER
1997

AUTOMATED
1913

OPERATOR
Associated British Ports

ACCESS
East Cote light is on the promenade north of the village, Lees Scar light can be seen on foot at low tide, but is best visited by boat

The creation of the port at Silloth came about with the formation of the Carlisle and Silloth Bay Railway and Dock Co in August 1856. The company built a railway extension into Silloth and in 1857 had a pier constructed from the west beach, after which the steamer service to Liverpool was transferred from Port Carlisle. In 1959 the company constructed the dock complex which is still in use, and Silloth became a planned town with its own port.

Details of lighthouses guarding the approaches to Silloth are scant, but it is believed that a wooden tower existed about 1,000 yards north of the harbour in 1841, although other records suggest 1864. Located on the foreshore adjacent to the roadway, it is sometimes called Skinburness, although its official name is East Cote Rear. It was one of a pair of leading lights with the front or Cote light mounted on a circular wooden tower on the south pier extension. The light was on a wooden pyramidal structure which was mounted on a short rail track so that it could be moved to accurately mark the channel into Silloth harbour.

In 1913 this wooden tower was replaced by a 39ft white square metal pyramid tower, which carried an electrically-powered fixed green light, visible for ten miles, in a white-painted corrugated-iron octagonal lantern room complete with a black conical room. Inside the base was a single-storey keeper's dwelling. The light was electrically operated and was automated in 1930. In 1997 Associated British Ports completely rebuilt it in a similar form but fixed in position on the short railway track and dispensed with the keeper's hut. The light is still operational and can be seen on the promenade.

The front East Cote light, originally mounted on the end of the dock pier, was a short hexagonal wooden tower with a lantern room complete with a conical roof above a circular shelter. The light and the pier were demolished in 1956, when the latter became unsafe. Today, a

▶▶ The light at East Cote, originally one of a pair of range lights, is north of Silloth harbour, which lies on the south side of the Solway Firth

▶ An old postcard showing the East Cote light with the keepers' dwelling.

Silloth

▶ The front East Cote light at the end of the pier at Silloth. Both the pier and the light were demolished in 1956.

▼ The pile lighthouse at Lees Scar, a submerged reef lying to the south-west of Silloth harbour.

14ft multi-use wooden structure on the south breakwater shows two fixed green lights.

About 800 yards south of the harbour, and 700 yards out to sea, was a 45ft pile lighthouse called Lees Scar, known locally as 'Tommy Legs'. It consisted of a cottage-style lighthouse with a circular lantern room on top of the keepers' accommodation, and showed the light through a window. A small boat, hung on davits, was used by the keepers to reach the shore. This light, which marked a submerged reef, was removed, but the pile legs were left in place and now hold a solar-powered green flashing navigation light on a 36ft pole. The structure is unsafe and its future is in doubt.

Isle of Man Lighthouses

Point of Ayre

Point of Ayre

Port Erin

Ramsey

Maughold Head

Peel

Douglas Harbour

Laxey Pier

Castletown

Douglas Harbour
Douglas Head

Port Erin

Castletown

Derbyhaven

Calf of Man

Port St Mary

Herring Tower

Thousla Beacon

Langness

Chicken Rock

N
W   E
S

0   4 m
0   4 km

The lighthouses on the Isle of Man can be categorised into two groups: the harbour lights operated locally, and the major lighthouses, which were built by and remain the responsibility of the Northern Lighthouse Board. The photographs show the lighthouses as they are today, and all, apart from the Calf of Man and Chicken Rock, can be easily visited.

Point of Ayre

The lighthouse at the Point of Ayre, on the northern tip of the Isle of Man, was built in 1818 and first lit in 1819. It was intended to obviate the dangers to vessels passing the Isle of Man along Scottish west coast routes, on routes to Ireland and heading for ports such as Liverpool. It is somewhat surprising that, at the turn of the nineteenth century, no lights had been built on the island to guide seagoing vessels, except for a number of small harbour lights.

Concerns had been expressed by mariners from Liverpool and other ports about the dangers of the Isle of Man and its headlands, notably the Point of Ayre and Calf of Man, remaining unmarked. However, proposals for major lighthouses only materialised at a meeting of the Commissioners for Northern Lights on 14 February 1814, when the idea for building a lighthouse at the Point of Ayre was discussed. A light on the Isle of Man would, with the newly planned light for Corsewall Point in Galloway, complete the lights for shipping using the Clyde.

As jurisdiction for lighthouses on the Isle of Man had not been given to any organisation, after consulting with the then owner of the Island, Duke of Atholl, the Commissioners for Northern Lights sought an Act of Parliament to authorise it to erect lighthouses at Point of Ayre and Calf of Man and charge dues to support them. Thus, the Isle of Man came under the auspices of Scotland's lighthouse board, rather than Trinity House.

Robert Stevenson, engineer to the Board, visited the island in 1815 at the behest of the Chief Magistrate of Greenock, and with the support of trade bodies on the Clyde. He was appointed engineer to the project, and set about surveying the area around Point of Ayre to find a suitable site for a lighthouse. He had to ensure that the foundations were built on solid ground, and that the position of a tower would be such that the encroaching sea did not become a problem.

As the Board was short of money, construction did not begin until 1817, after

▶▶ The impressive red and white lighthouse at Point of Ayre on the northern tip of the Isle of Man.

▶ An old postcard of Point of Ayre lighthouse and its associated buildings.

Point of Ayre

considerable efforts had been made to raise the necessary funding. By November 1818 the building work had been completed and the circular stone lighthouse was ready, together with its associated service buildings and keepers' dwellings. The tower was 98ft in height, painted white with two broad red bands, and was topped by the lantern with a gallery.

The light, which could be seen from the Mull of Galloway, had a range of nineteen miles and was a revolving catoptric consisting of fourteen parabolic reflectors, which revolved every two minutes and displayed a red light for one minute followed by a white light for one minute. No dues could be raised on the new lighthouse until the two lights on the Calf of Man were ready.

In 1890 the station was completely refurbished and a new lantern was installed, which reduced the height by a few feet. The new lantern was a first order Barbier & Bernard Fresnel dioptric equalising light, which revolved every eight minutes and produced an alternating red and white flashing light, each of thirty seconds duration. Although electricity was connected in 1955, the Chance Brothers paraffin vapour lamp was not replaced until 1978, when a 250-watt mercury vapour lamp was installed. Between 1991 and 1993 the station was automated, with the clockwork rotating mechanism replaced and the light up-rated to 400 watt.

The reflectors with the alternating red and white light were discontinued in the 1990s, and refractors were used to provide a quick flashing light with a range of twenty-one miles, showing four flashes every twenty seconds. Although the light was partially obscured as

Point of Ayre

it passed over a farmer's barn, the cows which had previously ignored the slow alternating light were distressed by the new quick flashes. The Board therefore agreed to increase the obscured area to solve the problem. Since automation, the associated buildings have become privately-owned holiday lets.

During the refurbishment in 1890, a single fog siren was installed in a 33ft concrete tower, with a large horn. In 1939 a second siren and horn was added, giving three blasts every ninety seconds, and the engines and compressors were replaced. In 1992 the sirens were replaced by an electric emitter and the character changed to three blasts every sixty seconds. The fog signal was discontinued in 2005.

Because of the continual build-up of shingle, the high light got further from the sea each year so, in 1889, a second smaller red octagonal cast-iron tower

was built 250 yards to seaward of the main tower. This 20ft light had a balcony and black lantern, a set of railings round the base, and a walkway was built across the beach. By 1950 the build-up of shingle required this smaller light to be resited a further 250ft to seaward, so a 15ft octagonal concrete tower, white painted with a black base slightly broader than the original tower, was built.

The original cast-iron tower, built by James Dove and Co, Edinburgh, was then erected on top. This gives the impression that the 35ft tower has two galleries, with the top section narrower than the bottom. The light was automated in 1993, when the original fifth order fixed lens, with an AGA flasher using acetylene gas, was replaced by a Tideline ML300 lantern with a sixty-watt bi-filament lamp showing a flashing white light with an eight-mile range. It was discontinued on 7 April 2010.

▶▶ The lower light, concrete fog signal tower and the lighthouse, from the pebble beach looking west.

▼ The keepers' cottages and maintenance buildings, with the lighthouse in the centre.

Ramsey

ESTABLISHED
circa 1766, North Pier
1800, South Pier 1845

CURRENT TOWER
North Pier 1864,
South Pier 1876

OPERATOR
IoM Government,
Department of
Transport, Harbours
Division

ACCESS
Both lights are
accessed via the
breakwaters

►► The South Pier
lighthouse (nearest
camera) is similar
to that on the
North Pier.

▼ The lighthouses at
the end of Ramsey's
two piers mark
the entrance to
the harbour.

The early history of lighthouses in Ramsey is not well chronicled, but a report of 1766 stated that a light existed there. But by 1790 the harbour was silting up, so a new south pier was constructed to augment the north pier and, in 1800, a 29ft lighthouse was built on the north pier. Between 1842 and 1843 a new 550ft north breakwater was built, which was extended in 1864, at which point a lighthouse was erected on its end.

The 23ft hexagonal cast iron tower with a hooded lantern shows a quick green flashing light which has a range of ten miles. Painted white at the top and black at the bottom, it is topped by an ornate weather vane. An interesting feature is the small spy hole in the rear of the partially enclosed lantern, which enables the harbour master to check that the light is lit.

In 1844 a temporary wooden lighthouse was erected on the end of the 440ft-long south pier. A year later this temporary light was replaced by a 28ft stone tower, which displayed a fixed white light that was visible for four miles. In 1851 the character was changed to fixed red.

In 1876 the south breakwater was constructed and the lighthouse that remains in use, manufactured by Bellhouse of Manchester, was erected on its end. Similar to the north light, it consists of a 23ft hexagonal cast iron tower with a hooded lantern, which shows a quick red flashing light with a range of ten miles.

The tower, topped by an ornate weather vane, is white with a red band at the top and black at the bottom. The lantern has a pane of glass in the rear to enable the light to be monitored. There is also a simple red pole on the pier which shows two fixed vertical red lights and is used by vessels once they are in the channel to the inner harbour.

Maughold Head

▶▶ The impressive lighthouse at Maughold Head, a rocky outcrop to the south of Ramsey.

▼ The keepers' dwellings, now privately owned, were built on the flat ground above the tower at Maughold Head.

Prior to 1914 the east coast of the Isle of Man was marked south of Point of Ayre by light vessels at Whitestone Bank and at Bahama Bank, off Ramsey Bay. But complaints were received that the Whitestone light was often extinguished and in 1909 a fog signal was requested for Maughold Head. Although Trinity House initially declined the request, it was eventually sanctioned and work to build a lighthouse began in 1912.

In order to get below the fog level, the 77ft white circular tower, designed by David A. and Charles Stevenson, was built into the sheer cliff face about 80ft below the cliff top, with the associated flat-roofed service buildings and two-storey keepers' dwelling above. It first exhibited a light on 15 April 1914

The Chance Brothers' incandescent burner was housed in a black dome roofed lantern room. Shown through a Fresnel lens, the light was group flashing white light, three flashes every thirty seconds, visible for twenty miles. Today the light is powered by two 250-watt multi-vapour lamps with a changeover, with an emergency lantern bolted onto the balcony.

A fog signal, giving one seven-second blast every ninety seconds powered by three diesel-engined compressors, was installed in 1914. The fog horn, located at the lighthouse base, was discontinued in 1987.

The station was connected to mains electricity in 1947 but because of the unreliability of the overhead network a standby system was also installed. Since then the lines have been replaced by underground cables. Mains water was connected in 1956 and the station now has a helipad. The station was automated in 1993, after which the keepers' dwellings and some of the service buildings were converted to private accommodation. During the conversion, the fog signal compressor and its associated equipment were removed.

Laxey Pier

ESTABLISHED
1851

CURRENT TOWER
Pier 1951,
Breakwater 1951

OPERATOR
IoM Government,
Department of
Transport, Harbours
Division

ACCESS
Both lights are
accessed via the pier
and breakwater

▶▶ The lights at
Laxey mark the
entrance to the
small harbour,
which is still used by
small pleasure craft.

▶ The harbour light
on the south pier
is shown from this
small white tower.

▼ The light on the
north breakwater.

Prior to 1780 Laxey, on the Isle of Man's east coast north of Douglas, was a small fishing village, but the discovery of zinc ore in great quantities led to the opening of Laxey mine, which by 1870 was reputedly the largest in the UK. In order to export the ore, the mining company built a harbour at the river mouth and, by 1851, a light was being displayed at this harbour.

The south side or Laxey Pier was completed first and it was probably here that the first light was displayed. The Isle of Man Examiner Annual Report of 1897 describes a tower showing a fixed white light, that was visible for four miles, still displayed from the old pier. In 1941 a 13ft stone tower, slightly tapering with a domed top, was erected on the end of the pier. Painted white with a red band, the occulting red light, visible for five miles, was displayed through a small window in the dome.

On the north side of the harbour is a substantive breakwater, which was built after the original pier. On the end is a light, almost identical to that on the south side, which shows an occulting green light and has a green band. No building date is known for this tower, but as it is so similar to the pier light it is likely to be of the same age. A spy hole in the rear of the dome enables the harbour master to monitor the light. Although commercial trade ceased at Laxey in 1973, the picturesque harbour is kept in pristine condition.

SWIMMING
STRICTLY
PROHIBITED
IN HARBOUR
AREAS

Douglas Harbour

ESTABLISHED
Early 1671

CURRENT TOWER
Early 1960s (Battery Pier)

OPERATOR
IoM Government, Department of Transport, Harbours Division

ACCESS
Battery Pier is open to the public

Douglas harbour is the main port for the Isle of Man, and throughout its history a series of aids to navigation has been erected as the port has been developed. Modern ferry travellers entering the harbour for the first time will see, having rounded Douglas Head, the tower at the end of Battery Pier. But this is only the latest and most prominent of the many harbour lights, of all shapes and sizes, that have been built around Douglas at various times.

Little information exists about early harbour lights, but in 1671 a great lantern with two lights was reportedly displayed to aid mariners. The harbour was very basic at this time, and this light was probably near the root of today's King Edward VIII Pier.

Throughout the eighteenth century the port was gradually developed, and part of the expansion saw the Harbour Commissioners erect a pier at the entrance to the port in 1758, at the end of which was built a brick lighthouse. The tower was completed in 1760 and was a fine stone built circular lighthouse. It was described at the time as a brick lighthouse, 'between thirty and forty feet high, lighted each night by seven or eight half-pound candles, with a tin circular reflector behind them of about eight feet diameter, and could be seen at the distance of four or five leagues at sea'.

However, in the summer of 1787 this lighthouse was completely destroyed, along with the pier, during a fierce easterly gale, which swept both pier and tower away. At this point, the only light in the harbour was an oil lantern on a pole at the extremity of the wrecked pier.

In 1793 work commenced on the Red Pier, which was situated at the root of today's King Edward VIII Pier and was completed at a cost about £24,000. It was 540ft in length and provided vessels in Douglas Bay with shelter from bad weather. In 1796 an elaborate 34ft round stone lighthouse was constructed on the end of this pier. The top castellated section was painted white with a black

▶▶ The lights at the end of Battery Pier at the entrance to Douglas harbour.

▶ The lighthouse on Red Pier was built in 1796 but is no longer standing.

Old Pier & Harbour, Douglas, I. O. M.

Douglas Harbour

▶ An old postcard of the entrance to Douglas harbour with Battery Pier on the right and Victoria Pier on the left.

▼ The lighthouse on Battery Pier seen from the ferry, with Douglas Head lighthouse behind.

conical dome and the light, which was visible for at least six miles, was exhibited through a window. This tower was demolished between 1929 and 1936 during work to replace the Red Pier with the King Edward VIII Pier.

Although not a light structure, the tower of refuge on Conister Rock just outside the harbour is a significant landmark for shipping in Douglas Bay. The building was completed in 1832 by the sea rescue pioneer Sir William Hillary, founder of the Royal National Lifeboat Institution, who was so concerned at the terrible loss of life in the bay that he had the castelled tower built. This tower stands as a testament to his great vision and foresight, and supports a simple quick flashing white light visible for four miles. Another of Sir William's plans

involved construction of a 'Great Central Harbour', which included a lighthouse at the end of one of the proposed piers. Although nothing came of these ideas, the harbour was later developed on lines broadly similar to those proposed in the plans.

In 1879 the Battery Pier, as it became known, was completed as part of improvements to the port, and it encloses the east side of the harbour. At its end is the 33ft tapered circular stone tower complete with a gallery and lantern, which is an impressive harbour light and was built in about 1960. Painted white with a horizontal red band, the tower houses a light which shows a quick flashing red light visible for one mile. It also carries a fog signal in the form of a bell.

Other aids to navigation around the harbour include small harbour lights on Victoria Pier, King Edward Pier, Fort Anne Jetty, Princess Alexandra Pier and the dolphin off this latter pier. The Victoria Pier light is mounted on the traffic control building, while the King Edward and Fort

Anne lights are green and red respectively, and they act as guides for the ferries which use the harbour.

The other significant aid to navigation for ships approaching the harbour is a pair of leading lights facing the harbour entrance, which have to be lined up for safe passage into port.

▲ The leading light in the centre with, background right, the light on the dolphin and, background left, Victoria Pier traffic control.

◀ The aids to navigation mounted on a pole by Victoria Pier traffic control.

Douglas Head

ESTABLISHED
1832

CURRENT TOWER
1892

AUTOMATED
1986

OPERATOR
Northern Lighthouse Board

ACCESS
A purpose-built footpath leads down from the A37 to the headland and lighthouse; entering the harbour on the ferry also offers good views of the station

Douglas is the modern capital of the Isle of Man, and is home to the largest of the island's ports. The town was developed during the Victorian era, and, today, is not only home to many hundreds of small craft but is also the terminal for the car and passenger ferries that run to the UK and Ireland.

The headland to the south of Douglas was a danger to shipping passing the island and entering the harbour, and it was first marked in 1811 when the British Government commissioned Thomas Brine to erect daymarks at Langness and Douglas. The beacons, identical 60ft cylindrical castellated stone towers, were never lit, and the one at Douglas was incorporated into the Douglas Head Hotel in 1869. Although the hotel was demolished to make way for flats in 1999, the tower was retained and can still be seen.

During the early years of the nineteenth century, as the harbour expanded and developed, several small aids to navigation were constructed in and around the port area, and a lighthouse was built on the headland in 1832 by the Harbour Board in the position occupied by the current light. The tower was 68ft in height but the fixed white light, visible for sixteen miles, was essentially a harbour light.

However, the Harbour Commissioners had insufficient funds to maintain it on a regular basis, as no dues were collected by them for the lighthouse, and by the 1850s it was inactive. As a result, negotiations began with the Commissioners for Northern Lighthouses for the taking over of the operation of the light, and in August 1857 it came under the control of the Board.

Following the takeover, the Commissioners implemented a number of improvements at the station, including extending the living accommodation so that two keepers and their families could live at the station. However, by the late 1880s the buildings that made up the station were in a poor state of repair, and due to their age needed constant repair and maintenance work,

►► The impressive lighthouse at Douglas Head is one of the island's best known landmarks.

► An old postcard of Douglas Head lighthouse with one of the Isle of Man Steam Packet's vessels heading away from the island.

THE LIGHTHOUSE, DOUGLAS. I. O. M.

Douglas Head

▶ Another old postcard view of Douglas Head with a Steam Packet vessel leaving harbour.

which was costly to implement. As a result, the Commissioners decided that the whole station should be rebuilt.

The engineers to the Board, David and Thomas Stevenson, designed a completely new lighthouse, including keepers' accommodation, which was built on the existing site. After obtaining permission from the Board of Trade for the new lighthouse in 1891, work began on it in early 1892. The tender for the construction work was awarded to Stratton, of Edinburgh. Milne & Son supplied the lantern and parapet, and Barbier & Co the dioptric apparatus. The machine, revolving carriage and lamps were supplied by Dove & Co, and a lens, which had 330 reflecting prisms, was made in France for £2,500.

The new station consisted of a 66ft round stone tower with a gallery and lantern, with single-storey flat-roofed castellated buildings on three sides, and the keepers' single-storey apex-roofed dwellings on the other side. The building materials had to be brought to the site by sea as no roads reached the station. Originally the lighthouse had two red bands, but in the early years of the twentieth century the tower was painted white with a buff gallery and a black lantern.

The light was initially powered by paraffin vapour with a fourth order catadioptric lens, with a character of six quick flashes over fifteen seconds, and a period of darkness of fifteen seconds. In 1986 the station was automated and converted to electrical operation. Today it has two double banks of twelve sealed beam units facing in opposite directions, turned by an AGA PRB21 Gearless Drive Unit giving a flash every ten seconds.

A fog signal in the form of a horn, known locally as 'Moaning Minnie', was commissioned in July 1908 but, following complaints, was re-sited round the headland. It was placed there at the request of the Harbour Board to assist the vessels reach port safely in poor visibility. The horn was later replaced by a siren but has since been discontinued.

▶▶ The tower is 68ft in height and the light has a range of twenty-four miles. In the event of a power failure, an emergency 200mm lantern is fixed onto the gallery and there is also a fixed red light on the radio mast.

Derbyhaven

Derbyhaven is a natural harbour north of Langness Point and is a small hamlet at the neck of the Langness peninsular. In about 1650 the first light on the Isle of Man was erected here to guide the herring fleet into the harbour. Mounted on a 30ft wooden structure, it was lit only during the herring season to help vessels return to Castletown, but how long the light was in operation for is unknown.

In 1842 the breakwater was constructed across the centre of the bay, and in 1850 the engineer James Gelling was appointed to erect a light on this breakwater. A lighthouse displaying a white light visible for two miles was built on the south-west end of the breakwater in 1897. It is not known if this light was still in existence in 1946 when the light in use today was constructed in the same location.

Along with the Laxey lights, the current light is similar to the Irish Quay light at Castletown and consists of a 12ft circular stone tower, painted white with a green horizontal band, complete with a domed top. The isophase green light is displayed through a window and a spy hole in the rear enables the light to be monitored from the land as the breakwater is only accessible on foot at low water.

At the entrance to Derby Haven is St Michael's Island, or Fort Island. On the island, which is a bird sanctuary, are two ruins, one of a church and the other a fort constructed by James, 7th Earl of Derby and Lord of Mannin in 1650. During the late eighteenth century a turret was raised on the east side as a lighthouse, which was lit from sunset to sunrise during the herring season.

▼ The small light on the breakwater at Derbyhaven.

Herring Tower

The first attempt to mark the headland at Dreswick Point, Langness, was made in 1811 when the British Government commissioned Thomas Brine to erect daymarks at Langness and Douglas. Two identical beacons were built, both 60ft cylindrical castellated stone towers, but whilst the one a Douglas was never lit there is a suggestion that the Langness tower at one time had what was described as a torch on its summit.

The tower has become known as the Herring Tower because a torch or flare was displayed during the herring season to guide the fishing boats into the nearby harbour of Derbyhaven.

ESTABLISHED
1811

CURRENT TOWER
1811

OPERATOR
Manx National Heritage

ACCESS
On the road to Langness lighthouse past the golf course, on ground to the west of the lighthouse

◀ The Herring Tower on Dreswick Point, near Langness, was built to carry a lighted flare to guide the herring fleet into Derbyhaven when that was a significant fishing port on the island.

Langness

▶▶ Langness
lighthouse stands
in the middle of the
keepers' buildings.

▼ Unlike the other
Isle of Man lights,
the buildings at
Langness were
fairly simple, having
roofs without
ornamental castling.

The small low-lying peninsula known as Langness is connected to the mainland by a narrow neck of land at the small village of Derbyhaven. Although the peninsula, which extends two miles out to sea, is a considerable hazard to the unwary mariner, the lighthouse was not built until 1880, several decades after the first Isle of Man lighthouses were constructed by the Commissioners for Northern Lighthouses. In 1801, during his tour of the British Isles, Robert Stevenson recommended to the Commissioners that a light should be established at Langness as a matter of urgency.

The tower, known as Herring Tower, was built in 1811, but it was not much use as an aid to navigation, and shipwrecks continued. During the twenty-five years before Langness was built, over forty shipwrecks were recorded in the area, with considerable loss of life as a result. Despite this, Trinity House,

who advised the Commissioners, could not be persuaded to build a light on Langness due to its prevalence to fog.

In the 1870s debates raged about the building of a lighthouse at Langness, as the Elder Brethren of Trinity House were reluctant to agree to any proposal. Instead, a red sector was employed at Chicken Rock, but this was not a success, while to the north, Douglas Head lighthouse was not in sight and could not be considered as a warning for Langness. Matters came to a head following further wrecks in the area, and with the invention of the fog signal to overcome the problem of mist, Trinity House sanctioned the building of a lighthouse as well.

By the end of 1877 plans had been drawn up for both a lighthouse and fog signal by the engineers David and Thomas Stevenson, and work began late the following year following delays caused in acquiring the

Langness

necessary land. Tenders were invited for the building of the new station, and the contract was awarded to Morrison & Sons, of Edinburgh, who tendered £3,979 7s 7d. The lantern was purchased from James Milne & Son at a cost of £621 10s 0d.

Construction proceeded during 1879 and 1880, and on 1 December 1880 the light was exhibited for the first time, with the fog siren buildings also ready for use. The 60ft white circular tower, complete with gallery and black lantern, was built in the centre of a courtyard with the keepers' houses, workshops and gas plant room surrounding the complex, which occupied an area two and a half acres in size, including the walled gardens.

When built, the new lantern emitted a flashing white light every five seconds and had a range of twenty-one miles. In December 1933 a fire broke out

in the lightroom destroying the lamps, but replacements were supplied and fitted by the keeper and his assistant. Following the fire, future requirements were considered and it was decided to upgrade the light.

In 1937 a new optical mirror apparatus was ordered from Messrs Parsons & Co at a cost of £561. Once this was ready, the lens for the petroleum vapour light source was then changed to a second order catoptric lens that used mirrors behind the light source instead of glass prisms. The character of the light was altered to a flash of one-third of a second every ten seconds.

Between 1994 and 1996 the station was automated and downgraded to a minor light. The optical apparatus installed in 1937 was removed and replaced by two 300mm lanterns in a biform arrangement and two sixty-watt bi-filament lamps

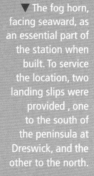

▼ The fog horn, facing seaward, as an essential part of the station when built. To service the location, two landing slips were provided , one to the south of the peninsula at Dreswick, and the other to the north.

showing two flashing white lights every thirty seconds with a range of twelve miles. The light operates from batteries charged from the mains supply and therefore does not require a standby generator. The station is the shore link for the Calf of Man and Chicken Rock lights.

The fog signal, situated on the shore to the south of the tower, consisted of a large horn housed in a concrete building with the air compressors housed outside, and feed pipes from the main buildings. It emitted two blasts every sixty seconds. It was deactivated in 1987, but is still in place today albeit unused.

In the summer of 1996 Langness was fully automated, and the keepers left. It was the last of the Northern Lighthouse Board's lighthouses on the Isle of Man to be demanned, and is now looked after by an attendant keeper. With the keepers gone, all but the tower and one small utility building were sold off, and today the accommodation has been converted into private holiday cottages.

▲ The lighthouse at Langness, similar in appearance to many Scottish lights, lies on a coastal footpath.

Castletown

ESTABLISHED
1765

CURRENT TOWER
Unknown

OPERATOR
IoM Government,
Department of
Transport, Harbours
Division

ACCESS
Both lights are
accessed via the
pier and breakwater,
which are open to the
public

► The red light
at the end of
the Irish Quay at
the entrance to
Castletown harbour.

In order to guide the herring fleet into the harbour at Castletown, the Isle of Man's first capital, a 16ft lighthouse was erected in 1765 at the harbour entrance. Exactly where this light was situated is unknown, but as it was shown whenever a ship entered harbour and throughout the herring season, it was probably on the end of what is now the Irish Quay.

Today, a 16ft circular stone lighthouse with a domed top,

which is a replacement for the original tower, stands on the end of this pier. White painted with a red band near the top, it shows an occulting red light visible for five miles every four seconds through a window.

In 1845 a new pier was built out from the west side of the Irish Quay to form the outer harbour, before an inner harbour had been excavated. In 1849 this pier was extended and a wooden lighthouse on legs was erected on the end. Today a 30ft circular stone tower, taller than the Irish Quay light and with a more ornate domed roof topped by a weather vane, stands at the end of this pier, displaying an occulting red light every fifteen seconds through a window.

The two lights form a transit to clear the training wall at the New Pier end. The channel into the inner harbour is marked on the north side by a green metal post on a concrete column showing an occulting green light every four seconds.

►► The light on
the new pier.

► The entrance
to the harbour is
marked by the light
on the Irish Quay
and a green light on
a concrete post on
the opposite side of
the channel.

Port St Mary Harbour

ESTABLISHED
1812

CURRENT TOWER
1886 (Alfred Pier)

OPERATOR
IoM Government,
Dept of Transport,
Harbours Division

ACCESS
The lights are
accessed via the piers

▶▶ The lighthouse
on the inner pier.

▼ The lighthouse
on Alfred Pier that
was washed away in
January 2009.

At Port St Mary a number of harbour lights have been built to help ships safely reach the quays that have been used at different times. When the inner pier was built in 1812, a 17ft lighthouse, which displayed a light visible for nine miles, was erected on the pier's end. In 1897 this served as one of the leading lights, working in conjunction with a fixed red light on a hill at the western side of the port.

The light is now housed in an octagonal cylindrical stone tower with a domed roof, painted white with a single horizontal red band, complete with a weather vane in the form of a fish on top. The light, which is displayed through a window, is occulting red every three seconds and has a range of five miles. There is a small window in the rear so the operation of the light can be monitored from the harbour.

In 1882 work began on enlarging the harbour with the building of a new breakwater, the Alfred Pier, on the end of which a fixed green light was erected. In 1892 this Pier was extended, and a new 23ft hexagonal cast-iron lighthouse, built by Edward Taylor Bellhouse, of Manchester, was erected on the extension. The light, which was transferred from Port Erin, was housed in a lantern topped by a fish-shaped weather vane. It showed a red occulting beam every ten seconds, visible for six miles. The light initially carried a fog bell, which sounded three blasts every twelve seconds when a vessel was expected, but it was disconnected in the 1990s.

Unfortunately the tower was destroyed and the harbour wall damaged during a severe gale on the night of 11 January 2009. All that remained the following day were a few metal stumps where the light had stood. The Isle of Man Harbour Authorities erected a temporary light within forty-eight hours. Situated in the same position, it has a six-mile range with the same character as the original tower. The two lights form a transit to enable vessels to clear the Carrick Rock, which presents a hazard to vessels from the east, and is marked by a 20ft black and red triangular tower.

Calf of Man

▶▶ The Calf of Man
High Light.

▼ The High Light
and the modern
light on the Calf of
Man as seen from
the sea.

The first lights built to mark the Isle of Man were at the Point of Ayre in the north and on the Calf of Man, a small island at Man's southern tip. The Isle of Man's central position in the Irish Sea presented a serious danger to vessels using the main west coast ports, such as Glasgow and Liverpool. As such, lighthouses were of key importance to many interested parties, including mariners based on the Mersey, as well as trade bodies on the Clyde.

The Commissioners for Northern Lighthouses gained an enabling act, passed on 7 June 1815 by the Houses of Parliament, to build aids to navigation on the Isle of Man. Although difficulties were experienced initially with the Duke of Atholl, owner of the Island, he eventually agreed to grant ten acres of land for the erection of dwellings, together with associated buildings. The tenant farmer on the Calf also objected, but his attempts to overturn the construction failed in the courts.

In 1817 work began on constructing two lighthouses on the island, which were lined up to mark the notorious Chicken Rock. About 300 men were employed during the summer of 1818, and Robert Stevenson was the engineer in charge. Sited 560ft apart, the lights were built at heights chosen so that the light beams coincided at the Rock. The high light was an unpainted 60ft circular stone tower with a gallery and a lantern, and a domed copper roof. A two-storey keepers' dwelling was connected to the tower by a single-storey service room. The low light was of similar design, but the tower was only 50ft in height.

Delays in construction work were caused by a storm in August 1818, which wrecked the supply boat on rocks in the Calf Sound. However, on 1

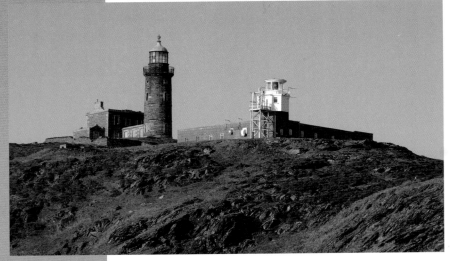

Calf of Man

As a result a lighthouse was built on the Rock itself, and once this was in operation, in January 1875, the two lights on the Calf were extinguished.

The keepers' dwellings were retained as a shore base until 1912, when the base was moved to Port St Mary. The Calf of Man had a new lease of life during the second half of the twentieth century, after a fire in Chicken Rock lighthouse in 1960 left the tower inoperable. A temporary light was shown from the low light on the Calf for two years following the fire.

After the fire, Chicken Rock was rebuilt as a minor light and a new major light was built on the Calf of Man. The building work was undertaken by Border Construction, of Whitehaven, who used a helicopter to move the necessary materials, as this was considered to be more

▲ The low light and the modern station looking towards Chicken Rock lighthouse.

▼ The Calf of Man low light. Four light keepers and their families lived on the Calf, as each lighthouse had both a principal and assistant keeper.

February 1819 the two lights were shown for the first time. The high light was 375ft and the low tower 282ft above high water. The high light had a range of twenty-four miles and the low light twenty-two miles. The towers displayed revolving white lights, which were kept synchronised by adjusting the clockwork drives. However, the high tower was often obscured by fog so the lights did not effectively mark Chicken Rock.

effective, in terms of both cost and time, than employing boats.

The modern light on the Calf, first lit in 1968, was situated between the old lights and consisted of a 35ft white-painted octagonal granite tower mounted on one end of a single-storey building. Accommodation was provided for four keepers, each of whom had their own bedroom. Twelve sealed beam units mounted on a gearless pedestal driven by a low voltage motor provided a flashing white light, which was visible for more than twenty miles. Electricity was provided by three diesel generators, any one of which could meet the station's needs.

In 1972 a helicopter landing pad was laid out close to the buildings, and in 1994 work was undertaken to automate the station. At this point, the optic was changed to a fourth order double catadioptric lens with a 250-watt metal halide lamp brought from the Barra Head lighthouse. The keepers were withdrawn on 22 March 1995, and an assistant keeper based in Port St Mary was appointed to carry out maintenance work. This arrangement lasted just over a decade until, following the upgrading of Chicken Rock, the light on the Calf was discontinued on 21 June 2007.

A Tyfon compressed air fog signal giving one blast every forty-five seconds was installed initially. This was changed to electric emitters in 1994, with a range of four miles, but was removed on 12 August 2005.

▲ The modern station was first lit in summer 1968. Almost 900 tons of building material was used to build the station, all of it moved by helicopter.

▼ The eight-sided concrete Thousla Beacon is situated in Calf Sound, and its red lantern has a range of nine miles.

Chicken Rock

▶▶ The impressive Chicken Rock lighthouse stands off the southern tip of the Isle of Man.

▼ The lighthouse was converted to solar power in 1999 and fitted with twin Tideland ML300 lanterns with halogen lamps in a lamp changer.

The Chicken Rock lies a mile to the south of the Calf of Man, and are the southernmost lands administered by the Isle of Man. Their location makes them a considerable danger to shipping, and so they were marked by a pair of leading lights on the Calf during the first half of the nineteenth century. However, fog often obscured these lights, so the Commissioners for Northern Lighthouses were granted permission to erect a light on the Chicken Rock itself.

Work on the rock began in 1870, but it was almost five years before the lighthouse was ready, in December 1874, and the light was first shown on 1 January 1875. Construction proved to be very challenging, as the Rock is virtually covered at high tide, while the tidal race made landing on it difficult. Work could only be carried out for about five hours each tide, and being swept off

the rock was a constant worry for the craftsmen employed.

David and Thomas Stevenson designed the unpainted tapering circular granite tower, which had a gallery and lantern complete with a black domed roof. The tower was built from granite stone blocks, which were shaped and prepared at a shore base in Port St Mary, a fishing village five miles away, before being transported to the rock. Initial estimates of the cost of the lighthouse were £46,000, but by the time the building was finished at least £20,000 more had been required.

The stone was brought from Dalbeatie in Scotland, and two steam tenders were used to transport materials to the rock. The first 32ft of the tower was built of sold granite masonry, and a bronze access ladder was fixed to the outside to reach the door. Seven storeys then led

Chicken Rock

from the entrance to the lantern machinery room, and then to the lantern itself and the structure was 143ft tall when finished. The keepers' accommodation consisted of two rooms with twin bunks, a kitchen and a living room. Each room was, of course, circular and no more than ten feet in diameter.

Throughout construction, considerable debate took place as to whether a red sector should be added to mark the Langness peninsular eight miles to the east. Stevenson was against this, but he was instructed to implement it despite his opinions. However, experiments proved him to be correct, and when the light went into service it was without the red sector. The optic, designed by Stevenson himself, was a dioptric holophotal system, and was an eight-sided frame with large annular lenses on each frame. It revolved round a paraffin vapour burner once every four minutes to give a flashing white light every thirty seconds, which was visible for twenty miles.

One of the conditions of building the station was that a fog signal be employed, so, on commissioning, two fog bells were rung every thirty seconds at times of pooh visibility. In 1890 the bells were replaced by a Tonite fog signal, and in 1911 a modern fog horn, which was much louder, was installed for use in poor visibility. The old bell was removed and became the church bell at St Catherine's Church in Port Erin.

The most dramatic event to take place at the lighthouse occurred on 23 December 1960 when a disastrous fire engulfed the lighthouse, rendering it inoperable. The keepers were saved by the Port St Mary lifeboat, in very difficult weather conditions, having had a lucky escape after being trapped at the top of the burning tower.

Following the fire, with the lighthouse out of action, a temporary light was displayed from the old Calf of Man light until 1962, by when the lighthouse had been repaired,

▶ The shore station for Chicken Rock built at Port St Mary in 1886. Initially the accommodation at Calf of Man lighthouses was used as a shore base, but in 1912 this was transferred to Port St Mary Shore Station until the lighthouse was demanned. This building was sold in 1995 after the Calf of Man lighthouse was automated.

re-equipped and automated. The new fourth order catadioptric lens and propane gas burner gave a flashing white light every five seconds with a range of thirteen miles. By 1968 the light had been supplemented by a new major light on the Calf of Man and Chicken Rock was redesignated a minor light. Following the fire a temporary foghorn was utilised until 1968 when a permanent fog horn,

giving two blasts every sixty seconds, was installed. It was discontinued in June 2005.

In 1999 the light was converted to solar power and in June 2007 it was upgraded to give a range of twenty-one miles. The two lights in alignment on Calf of Man were thus no longer required, and Chicken Rock, which is monitored via a radio link to Langness lighthouse, became a major light again.

▲ The Chicken Rock lighthouse with the two old lights on the Calf of Man pointing towards it. The 1968 lighthouse on the Calf is to the left.

Port Erin

▶▶ The 36ft
tower on the beach
housing the front
light at Port Erin.

▼ View over Port
Erin town and the
beach with the
leading light.

Although Port Erin is one of the less well developed of the Island's harbours, in 1876 an attempt was made to provide a harbour facility which saw a large breakwater built on the south side of the bay. A lighthouse was erected on the end of this breakwater which, it is believed, was subsequently transferred to Port St Mary. The project was ill-fated when, in 1881, the breakwater was completely destroyed in bad weather.

In 1884 a black buoy was placed at the end of the ruins and a pair of leading lights was placed at the rear of the bay to mark a safe transit clear of the hazard. The Front Range, which stood on the beach, consisted of a 34ft square concrete open lattice tower with a black metal hexagonal lantern; the Rear Range light was mounted on a concrete pole on the promenade.

The Front Range was subsequently replaced by a 36ft octagonal white concrete tower with a red band, a small gallery and a lantern, in the same location on the beach. It displays a fixed red light, which is visible for five miles. The current Rear Range, much altered since 1884, consists of a street lamp on a 15ft pole on the promenade. Painted white with a red central band, it supports two polycarbonate lamp holders showing fixed red lights visible for five miles.

In 1912 the short pier, which is known as Raglan Pier, was erected near to the base of the ill-fated 1884 breakwater, and a lighthouse was built to mark the pier in 1916. This light, which is still in operation today, consists of a 23ft concrete skeleton tower with a gallery and a tall domed lantern. The structure, which

Port Erin

is painted white with a green gallery and lower lantern, is topped with an ornate weather vane and can be seen from vantage points around the bay. The occulting green light flashes every seven seconds and is visible for five miles.

Something that may impinge on navigation in the area, and hence the light dispositions, is the use of redundant marine cable to create an artificial reef in the Port Erin Closed Area. An investigation into this has been proposed by the Department of Agriculture, Fisheries and Forestry. It is hoped that a variety of structures, to be monitored for a three-year period, will be colonised by marine life and will become an attraction for divers.

► The small light on Raglin Pier Head on the waterfront at Port Erin.

Peel harbour has a number of minor lights intended to help vessels to safety. Originally the harbour was centred around the river, but it was expanded to accommodate more vessels, and the original harbour area is now the inner harbour. The pier to the east of the river was washed away twice in the eighteenth century, but in 1809 it was strengthened and lengthened. The following year a fixed red light, 21ft above high water and with a range of eight miles, was erected on the end. This, the first light in the harbour, was built after severe criticism at the lack of aids to navigate into the port.

In 1861 a new light was erected on the pier head. Today the light is mounted on the top of the white-stoned old harbour masters office and consists of a simple solar powered polycarbonate lamp on a small round stone pedestal. It shows a red occulting light every seven seconds, which has a range of eight miles.

To the west of the inner harbour, under the castle, is Castle Jetty, which was constructed in 1829 but there is no record of a lighthouse being built to mark it at that time. However, a small 13ft circular masonry tower with a small domed lantern was subsequently built on this jetty. The tower may

ESTABLISHED
1810

CURRENT TOWER
Breakwater 1896, others unknown

OPERATOR
IoM Government, Department of Transport, Harbours Division

ACCESS
The lights can be viewed by walking the pier, jetty and breakwater

◄ The pier head light is mounted on top of the harbour control building.

▼ The Castle Jetty light and breakwater light at the entrance to Peel harbour.

Peel

date from the nineteenth century but the aluminium dome was a later addition. An occulting white light every seven seconds and visible for six miles shows from the lantern.

The most significant light in Peel was established on the breakwater that extends out from St Patrick's Island to form the outer harbour in 1856. In 1896 the breakwater was substantially lengthened and the current lighthouse was erected on the end. This light is displayed from an octagonal cast iron tower with a gallery and an elongated lantern topped by a weather vane. The occulting white light, visible for eight miles, flashes every seven seconds. When commissioned it carried a fog bell which was rung every fourteen seconds when vessels were expected, but it was discontinued in the mid-1990s.

A small light is mounted on the end of the groyne, which extends westward from the pier head, and consists of a simple solar-powered polycarbonate lamp mounted on a pole supported by a circular concrete column. It originally showed an occulting red light every two seconds, but in 2005 it was altered to a flashing red light every five seconds and at the same time a new light was established on the roof of the pumping station on the promenade. This solar-powered light also shows a flashing red light every five seconds and, with a visibility of eight miles, forms a transit with the groyne light to mark an obstruction out to sea.

Glossary

▲ The distinctive cast-iron light at Maryport dates from the middle of the nineteenth century.

▲ Walney Channel Pickle Scar light is one of several similar leading lights marking the entrance to Barrow in Furness port.

Acetylene A highly combustible gas which burns with an intensely bright flame.

Argand lamps A bright and relatively clean-burning lamp invented by Francois-Pierre Ami Argand in 1783.

Automated An unmanned light controlled externally; all the major UK lighthouses are automated with Trinity House controlling and monitoring its lights from the Corporation's Depot in Harwich.

Beacon A structure, usually land based, either lit or unlit, used to guide mariners.

Characteristic The identifying feature of a lighthouse is its characteristic; for example the light could be described as fixed, or flashing.

Daymark Light towers often also serve as daymarks, landmarks that are visible from the sea during daylight acting as aids to navigation.

Dioptric lens A development by Augustin Fresnel consisting of a bull's eye lens surrounded by a series of concentric glass prisms. Dioptric lenses were classified by their focal length.

Elevation The elevation refers to a light's height above sea level; the higher the elevation, the greater the range.

Flashing light A light where the period of light is less than the period of darkness.

Fog signals A sound signal used to warn mariners in times of fog or heavy weather.

Gallery A walkway beneath the lantern room to enable access for maintenance.

High light The taller or higher of a pair of lights.

Isophase light A light where the periods of light and dark are equal.

Keepers The persons responsible for maintaining and keeping the light at an aid to navigation, including the associated buildings.

Lanby The abbreviated term for Large Automatic Navigation Buoy, a modern floating unmanned aid to navigation often used in place of a ligthship.

Lanterns The glass-enclosed space at the top of a lighthouse housing the lens or optic; lanterns are often encircled by a narrow walkway called the gallery.

Lightship A vessel powered or unpowered designed to support a navigational aid.

Low light The shorter or lower of the two lights used to mark a channel or hazard.

Occulting Where the period a light exhibited is greater than its period of eclipse; this can be achieved in several ways.

Range lights Lights displayed in pairs which are used to mark a navigable channel.

Reflector A system which intensifies light by reflecting the light source into a beam, both to increase intensity and to enable the beam to be manipulated to produce differing light characteristics.

Training wall A bank or wall erected below water level in a river or harbour mouth to train the water flow.

Appendix

Bibliography

Hague, Douglas B. and Christie, Rosemary: Lighthouses: Their Architecture, History and Archaeology (Gomer Press, Dyfed, 1975).

Hellowell, John: A Tour of Manx Lighthouses (Peter Williams Associates, Milford Haven, Pembrokeshire, 1998)

Jackson, Derrick: Lighthouses of England and Wales (David & Charles, Newton Abbot, 1975)

Medlicott, Gordon: Discovering Lighthouses: A tour of discovery along the coast of Lancashire & Cumbria (2003)

Nicholson, Christopher: Rock Lighthouses of Britain (Patrick Stephens, Somerset, 1995).

Sutton-Jones, Kenneth: To Safely Guide Their Way: Lighthouses and Maritime Aids of the World (B&T Publications, Southampton, 1998).

Woodman, Richard and Wilson, Jane: The Lighthouses of Trinity House (Thomas Reed Publications, 2002).

▲ The lighthouse at Hale Head built in 1906, with the gallery round the lantern visible.

Websites

www.alk.org.uk The Association of Lighthouse Keepers provides a forum for all those interested in lighthouses.

www.lighthousedepot.com Detailed list of world lights with photos and locations.

www.trabas.de/enindex.html List of world lights including minor lights with photos.

www.trinityhouse.co.uk Trinity House website with details of all their lighthouses.

www.michaelmillichamp.ukgateway.net Contains details of operational and non-operational lights.

www.nlb.org.uk Northern Lighthouse Board, which maintains lighthouses around Scotland and the Isle of Man.

www.isle-of-man.com/manxnotebook/maritime/lighthse/hlights.htm Includes a history of harbour lights on the Isle of Man.

▲ The unique screw-piled Wyre light at the entrance to the port of Fleetwood.

Acknowledgements

A number of people have assisted with the compilation of this book. The following helped in various ways. The pioneering research into Isle of Man lights by John Hellowell has proved extremely useful and we are very grateful for his considerable assistance. David Forshaw, Michel Forand, John Mobbs and Fred Fox assisted with various images. Thanks also to John Curry and Gerry Douglas-Sherwood.

All photographs and images are by Nicholas Leach, except the following: Tony Denton pages 12, 46, 50, 62 (lower), 76; Michel Forand 11 (lower), 6, 7 (lower), 23, 24, 26, 27, 34, 36, 40; David Forshaw 29; Tony Lakin 1, 89, 101; Les Holt 35 (lower); John Hellowell 95, 96, 97 (upper); John Mobbs 76, 109 (upper). Finally, our thanks and gratitude to both Maureen and Sarah for their patience during our researches.

▲ The lighthouse at New Brighton when in service, built with a gallery round the lantern.

Index

Other books in this series

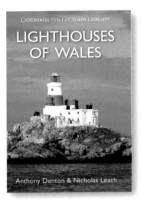

Lighthouses of Wales

The first volume in the series contains details of all the significant aids to navigation around the coast of Wales, from the Bristol Channel in the south to the Dee estuary in the north. As well as many high quality previously unpublished photographs, it contains histories of all the lighthouses and details of their locations, what access is possible for the visitor, and current use. The famous lighthouses covered include the offshore stations at Skerries and Smalls, the magnificent Nash Point towers, and the historic lighthouse at Mumbles Head.

£7.99 • Paperback • 96 pages • ISBN 9781843064596

Lighthouses of England: The North East

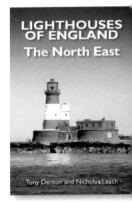

The north east volume contains details of all the lighthouses in Northumberland, Surham, Yorkshire and along the banks of the Humber. Many high quality photographs of the lighthouses are included, together with histories of all the lights, both major and minor, as well as details of their locations, visitor access and current use. Some of the lighthouses covered in this volume are Longstone, Souter, Whitby, Withernsea and Spurn Point, as well as the smaller lights in the Humber Estuary and the major ports.

£9.99 • Paperback • 96 pages • ISBN 9780951365663

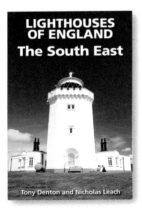

Lighthouses of England: The South East

The south east volume contains details of all the lighthouses in Norfolk, Suffolk, Essex and Kent. Many high quality photographs of the lighthouses are included, together with histories of all the lights, both major and minor, as well as details of their locations, visitor access and current use. Some of the lighthouses covered in this volume are Cromer, Lowestoft, Orfordness, North Foreland, South Foreland and Dungeness, as well as the unusual lights on the river Thames and in the Thames Estuary.

£9.99 • Paperback • 96 pages • ISBN 9780951365670

Available direct from
Foxglove Media, Foxglove House, Shute Hill, Lichfield WS13 8DB
t > 01543 673594   e > foxglove.media@btinternet.com